PAGES FROM THE
BIOGRAPHY OF AN EXILE

Adnan al-Sayegh
PAGES FROM THE
BIOGRAPHY OF AN EXILE

Translated by Stephen Watts &
Marga Burgui-Artajo

with an introduction by
Stephen Watts

PUBLICATIONS
2016

Published by Arc Publications,
Nanholme Mill, Shaw Wood Road
Todmorden OL14 6DA, UK
www.arcpublications.co.uk

978 1910345 18 4 (pbk)
978 1910345 19 1 (hbk)
978 1910345 20 7 (ebk)

Design by Tony Ward
Cover design by Tony Ward & Ben Styles
Printed in Great Britain by
TJ International, Padstow, Cornwall

Cover painting by Karim al-Wali (Iraq / USA)
by kind permission of the artist

ACKNOWLEDGEMENTS
The translators are grateful to *Exiled Writers Ink* and
the editors of *Long Poem Magazine* and *Agenda* for publishing
some of these poems previously in translation.
Stephen Watts would also like to acknowledge the support of
Arts Council England for a grant in 2009 that *inter alia* helped
support his work on at least some of these translations.

'Arc Translations'
Series Editor: Jean Boase-Beier

CONTENTS

Introduction & Translator's Note / 7

Adnan al-Sayegh, one of the foremost poets of the so-called Eighties Movement in Iraq, was born in al-Kufa close to the Euphrates in 1955. Other poets of his generation include Dunya Mikhail, Razaq al-Rubaie, Jawad al-Hattab, Fadel Jabr and Amal al-Jubouri, all of them coming of age during the Iran-Iraq war of the 1980s and all subsequently living in their poetic maturity through times of seemingly endless war and political danger. Many of them have had to seek safer lives in exile outside Iraq and, for al-Sayegh, this meant constant journeying, initially to a variety of Arab cities for many short stays, then to Sweden, and finally, since 2004, to London. Like Saadi Yussef, he moved from place to place, noting his temporary home under many of his poems.

Al-Sayegh became a poet early on. When he was 10 and his father fell ill, he found himself writing – and then hiding – what his mother, when she found it, called a poem, his first. As a child he was also in the habit of taking books to the shores of the Euphrates and while swimming, reciting 'poems' that he made up, as if talking to a friend in the water – a lovely metaphor for poetry as water, warmth and language. But because at the time he made these poems in colloquial, rather than classical, Arabic he only came to think of them as poems much later. His life as a child in al-Kufa with his family and his closeness to the Euphrates were vital to his development, but other factors were also at work. Kufa was the home town, for instance, of al-Mutanabbi, one of the very greatest of classical Arab poets.

Al-Sayegh began visiting Baghdad to stay with his uncle and the journeys he made took him close by Babylon. The 150-kilometre ride from Kufa to Baghdad became suffused with language and inspired his sense both of poetry as journey and of the physicality of words. At the age of 15, he became aware of the life and work of Da'abel al-Khazai, a rebel poet of the Abbassid period and in Kufa he made friends with Ali-al-Ramahi, a young and outspoken poet who was killed in 1979 at the hands of the government. Al-Sayegh's background and the influence of these two poets – the one classical, the other his contemporary – fostered in the aspiring poet the sense of being 'at a distance', an outsider. In particular he felt that al-Ramahi's 'blood energies' fed into his own poetic self and arrived at the belief that it is poetry that holds the possibility of change; rather than joining a political party (something that he's never done), being a poet might be the best way of directing and focusing political anger.

In 1976 his father died and al-Sayegh had to discontinue his studies. In 1980 the long and bloody war with Iran began and the young poet was conscripted, remaining twelve years in military service. These were among the most difficult times of his life and the most sorrowful; he felt his youth pulled away from him and many of his friends and companions were killed. In a real sense, these years of war fast matured him as a person and as a poet. He did not fit well with military authority and in 1984, together with a handful of colleagues, he was confined to a stable in Sheikh Osal near Sulaymania, close to the Iranian border, as a punishment. At this time his first book of poetry was published in Baghdad to critical acclaim, although he wasn't aware of its publication. By chance another soldier turned up with a newspaper containing both a photograph and an article about the book. Adnan says that he began there and then to write the first fragments of what became his *magnum opus*, the 500-page *Uruk's Anthem*. This work (of which two fairly short fragments are included in the present book) sums up his poetry's essence, the fractured and fratricidal struggles of modern Iraq, and his own life's trajectory.

Between the publication of his first book in 1984 and 1993, when he was forced to leave Iraq, he published six further books of poetry. The war with Iran formally ended in August 1988 and he was allowed to leave the army the following year. But his poetry was beginning to get him into trouble: his books *Sparrows Don't Love Bullets* and *Sky In A Helmet* were in effect banned by Saddam Hussein's government and disappeared from the bookshops. He himself managed to avoid arrest, but when in 1993 the theatre director Hamid al-Ghanem and the actors adapted a play for his company from sections of *Uruk's Anthem*, al-Ghanem was 'advised' to work with less questionable poetry and the poet felt under pressure to flee his home. Invited to the 'Jeresh' Poetry Festival in Jordan a few months later, al-Sayegh took the opportunity not to return to Iraq and six months later his wife and two young sons also managed to leave and join him in exile. Thus began their years of journeyings.

His first book published from exile, *Under A Strange Sky*, had an introduction by Saadi Yussef, thus further alienating him from the Iraqi government. It is worth saying again that the close-knit group of writer-friends in Baghdad in the late '80s and early '90s – including Dunya Mikhail, Razaq al-Rubaie, as well as al-Sayegh – all ended up leaving Iraq. The co-ordinates of al-Sayegh's poetry show him passing through many cities: by early 1996 al-Sayegh was in Beirut and it was there, in that year, that *Uruk's Anthem* was first published. Both poet and publisher were threatened and the poet was placed on a public death-list by Uday Hussein, after which the UN rapidly helped the poet and his family find formal asylum in Sweden in the winter of 1996, at first in the north – as the poet said, they went from 36 degrees plus to 36 degrees minus in a matter of hours. There, in remote, freezing Luleå, he felt himself spiritually shaken and wrote the poem 'The Deleted Part'. In May 1997 they moved south to the somewhat warmer city of Malmö where the poet remained until 2004 and wrote many of his best poems. He also got to know a number of Swedish writers, including Tomas Tranströmer, whom he'd already read in Arabic translation and who he first met in 1999, remaining on close terms until the Swedish poet's death in March 2015. His own poetry has been translated into Swedish, with two books being published in Malmö in 1997 and 2010 respectively. He has also remained in close contact with poet-friends such as Lasse Sandberg, Maria Lindberg, Arne Zaring and Karin Lentz and returns to Sweden from time to time to take part in readings there.

In 2004 he moved to London where he has lived ever since and where he has managed to carve out some sense of home. He notes certain similarities between London and Baghdad; both cities, for instance, have rivers flowing through their hearts that are crucial to their lives and both have red double-decker buses of very similar design. London is also a significant centre of Arabic culture, with newspapers, bookshops, publishing houses, journals and cafés, and it's worth noting that a number of Iraqi writers (and poets especially) have made their exiled homes in London. The 10-page 'Rain In London' was his first poem to be written here – as he fondly notes 'in the café of a Borders bookshop' – although this and many other of his London poems still await translation, together with the main body of *Uruk's Anthem*. He has worked alongside a number of UK poets, translating some into Arabic, and interpreting versions around the epic and legacy of Gilgamesh, particularly with the poet Jenny Lewis. His work has also been translated into English in North America by various poets and scholars, and into a number of other languages, Spanish, Dutch and Farsi among them.

He has read his work, often in translation, many times in London and more widely through Britain: at London's Poetry Café, the StAnza Festival, in Glasgow, at Ledbury, at the National Portrait Gallery (where he was recorded) and most recently, in July 2015, at Poetry International at the South Bank Centre. At the same time he frequently reads at festivals throughout Europe, Latin America and the Arab worlds: at the 1997 Rotterdam International Festival, in Medellin and in Cuba, to give a few instances. In October 2015, he read in Tokyo, and then in April 2016, he was invited to Iran for two weeks to celebrate the publication of a volume of his selected poems in Farsi – a visit of particular significance in the light of his previous experiences in the Iran-Iraq War some thirty years earlier.

Poetry is a way of life, a breathing existence for al-Sayegh in ways not true of every poet; he has at times wanted to say that poetry is his religion, but for the delusion of language in such a form of words. He would want it said that religion is far less important an expression of the human spirit than is poetry – he points to his first and enduring love for his fellow townsman al-Mutanabbi, to the street named after that poet in Baghdad, to the quote from Rilke on a Baghdad wall and the handwritten quote he had above his desk in Sweden. But such feelings and affiliations – including the affiliation to no religion – have got him into trouble throughout his life. The last time he was in Basra, having been invited in 2006 to the al-Marbed Poetry Festival, he was threatened with having his tongue cut off and thus forced into hasty and dangerous flight. Reading the poems in this book we come to understand that poetry is a vital act and that words of truth and testament have to be written, whatever the consequences.

A note on the Translation

The English texts in this book are co-translations, the result of three people working closely together. First Marga Burgui-Artajo would make very detailed word-by-word literals, checking many interpretations directly with the poet, which she then brought to me and the two of us – sometimes with Adnan present as well – would go very carefully through her literals sifting what might be the clearest meanings, while keeping a weather eye open to the best sounding text in English. These two initial stages were vital to establish accuracy while pointing the language of the translation towards a living breath. Then I would work on the poem on my own and send the updates to Marga, and we would meet once again to talk this second draft through towards the poem's final version. This was the process we went through with each poem or sequence of poems. Adnan also often provided recordings of himself reading so we would have the rhythm – as well as other less tangible auras of the poems – to hand if needed. The fact that all three of us were, and still are, living in London, and were able to meet with relative ease was also a vital part of this process. To see the text emerge from one language into the other in the physical presence of those involved is very important, not least because a great deal is sensed by being able to see words emerge from the body, as well as working with those words on the page. We were also much helped by being able to 'test' out our translations at bilingual readings, of which Adnan and I have given many from 2008 until now. It matters a lot to read and perform poems aloud and to be aware of the reactions of those listening. You can sometimes sense the solidity or frailty in the meaning or rhythm of what you have written in translation. Twenty three of these poems, mostly shorter ones but with a number of longer ones, including 'The Deleted Part of "Risalat al-Ghufran"', were first published as a chapbook by Exiled Writers Ink in 2009, and again it helped a lot to see these poems in print, to weigh their 'value' so to speak against the heaviness of the page. Similarly when the *Long Poem Magazine* published sections 1-16 of 'Pages of an Exile' in 2012 and we had the chance to do readings from this sequence in London, Glasgow, Cambridge and elsewhere, we were again able to listen to the weight of our words in the air and sense the balance of their light. We always aimed for close literal adherence together with clarity and light in the English: the two after all are not at all incompatible. We also always remained open to breaking the English, because while one value of translation may be to transport literal meaning, another aim, equally vital, is to test the new language and if necessary to rupture it. All languages live by renewal and change, and good translation might be part of this by aspiring to both lucid ease and sharp intakes of breath.

Arabic poetics underwent a thorough and complex revolution in the late 1950s and early 1960s, due partly to the efforts of Salah Abd al-Sabur in Egypt, the visionary movement around the magazine *Shi'r* led by Adonis and Yusuf al-Khal mostly in Beirut, and with the poetry of Badr Shakr al-Sayyab and others in Iraq. These movements – and others, since change is complex and happens over a long period of time – opened Arabic poetry up to modernism and free verse, and re-affirmed the historically natural poetic of prose and of fractured rhythms within Arabic poetry. Adnan al-Sayegh's poetry of course reflects this, down to his grammar and punctuation with its use of multiple dots and ellipses. We hope that we've managed to translate many of the qualities of al-Sayegh's work and that this book reflects something of the nature of exile in his poetry together with the speed and necessarily fractured nature of his poetics.

We're particularly grateful to Mouthanna al-Sayegh and Dana Nasser for their editorial help and to Angela Jarman & Tony Ward at Arc Publications for enabling this current larger bilingual selection of our work to be published. We hope that the sometimes strongly un-English qualities of Adnan al-Sayegh's poetry may impinge a little on current English poetry and poetics.

Stephen Watts
Whitechapel, June 2016

PAGES FROM THE
BIOGRAPHY OF AN EXILE

سماء في خوذة

أرتبكتُ أمام الرصاصةِ
كنّا معاً
في العراءِ المسجّى على وجهِهِ،
خائفين من الموتِ
جمّعتُ عمري في جعبتي،
ثم قسّمتهُ:
بين طفلي..
ومكتبتي..
والخنادق

(للطفولة، يتمي..
ولامرأتي، الشعرُ
والفقرُ..
للحربِ، هذا النزيفُ الطويلُ...
وللذكرياتِ.. الرمادْ)
وماذا تبقى لكَ الآنَ من عمرٍ
كنتَ تحملهُ – قلقاً – وهرولٌ بين الملاجيءِ والأمنياتِ
تخافُ عليه شظايا الزمان
قالَ العريفُ:
هو الموتُ
لا يقبلُ الطرحَ والجمعَ
فاخترْ لرأسكَ ثقباً بحجمِ أمانيكَ
هذا زمانُ الثقوبْ...
أوْ...
فأهربِ

الآنَ..
من موتكَ المستحيلْ
(– لا مهربٌ...
هي الأرضُ أضيقُ مما تصورتُ
... أضيقُ من كفِّ كهلٍ بخيلِ...
فمَنْ ذا يدلّ اليتيمَ على موضعٍ آمنِ

16

THE SKY IN A HELMET

I was bewildered before the bullet –
both of us together
there beneath the flattened sky,
                              dreading death
I gathered my life's pieces into my rucksack
                 and portioned them out:
                              for my son
                       for my library
                 for the trenches

(for childhood, an orphaning …
and for my woman, poetry
                       and poverty
for the war, this chronic bleeding …
and for memory … just ashes).
Now what is left to you of the life
you used to carry between bunker and hope,
always fearing this shrapnel of time.
The sergeant said:
This is death and
it doesn't deal in addition, subtraction,
so choose a hole the size of your desire,
this is the time for holes and for heads
or …
run for it

right now
              from such impossible death
(for there's no way out
the earth is narrower than we thought
narrower than that miser's palm …
and who'll take the orphan to safety

وقد أظلمَ الأفقُ..
وأسّودَ وجهُ الصباحْ)
....
ولا بأسَ..
كوّمتُ ما قد تبقى من السنواتِ البخيلةِ
ثم اندفعتُ...
– إلى أينَ....؟!
بينكَ والموتِ، فوهةٌ لا تُرى
وتساؤلُ طفلين:

– «بابا، متى ستعودُ..؟»
انكفأتُ،...
فصاحَ عريفي: هو الوطنُ الآنَ......
فأربَحفَ القلبُ من وهنٍ أبيضٍ
واختنقتُ بدمعةٍ ذلي:
– يا سماءَ العراقِ..
                   أما من هواءٍ
تلفّتُ..
كانتْ سماءُ العراقِ مثقّبةً بالشظايا
وكانتْ...........
....
تعثّرتُ في صخرة
فرأيتُ حذائي المُمزقَ يسخرُ مني...
(– لا بأسَ...
فليكتبِ المتخمون وراءَ مكاتبهم

... عن لحومِ الوطن)
....
في غرفةٍ، قبل عشرين
كانتْ ترتّقُ – في وجلٍ – بنطلوني العتيقَ
وتمسحُ ذلتها بالدموع
....

18

where the horizon goes dark
and the face of morning blacks out.)
. . . .
No worries.
I piled together what was left of me
and charged ahead
– but where to?
Between you and death there's an invisible muzzle
and the question two small children asked:

'Daddy, when are you coming back?'
I turned round …
The sergeant yelled, 'This is your homeland now …'
my heart shuddered, white with weakness
I choked with tears of humiliation:
O sky of Iraq
                is there air to breathe?
I looked everywhere.
Iraq's sky was punctured with shrapnel
and it was …
. . . .
I tripped on a rock
saw my burst boot laughing at me
(No worries …
let the fat clerks who sit behind their desks write

                … about the fat of the land)
. . . .
In a room, twenty years ago
She used – fearfully – to mend my worn trousers
Washing off her shame with her tears
. . . .

- أبي، أين يوميتي...؟!
الصحابُ مضوا لمدارسهم...
....
(الصحابُ مضوا للرصاص
والزمانُ أصمْ...)
الصحابُ...
الصحابُ...
الصـ...
سقطتُ...

فلملمني وطني...
وركضنا إلى الساتر الأول
نتحدى معا موتنا
- أيّنا سيختيّءُ
يا وطني -
رأسَهُ...؟
ولنا خوذةٌ...

واحدة

بغداد 1986

شيزوفرينيا

في وطني
يجمعني الخوفُ ويقسمني:
رجلاً يكتبُ
والآخرَ - خلفَ ستائرِ نافذتي -
يرقبني

بغداد 10/01/1987

20

'Father, where is my pocket money?'
My friends have gone to school already
....
(My friends have gone to their bullets
such destinies are deaf)
My friends
my friends …
my fri …
I fell …

and my homeland gathered me in
and we raced to the barricade
challenging death together.
Which of us will protect –
O my homeland –
                    his own head?
We have just one helmet

just one.

Baghdad 1986

SCHIZOPHRENIA

In my homeland
fear gathers me up and pulls me apart:
a man who writes
and another who watches over me
from behind closed curtains

Baghdad 10/01/1987

غيمة الصمغ

أقولُ: غداً
أتمدّدُ فوقَ النهارِ الفسيح
يظلّلني الغيمُ لا الطائراتُ
أفتشُ بين القنابلِ والطين
عمّا تبقى من العمرِ والأصدقاءِ
أعيّيءُ في رئتيَّ الشوارعَ والياسمينَ
وأمضي إلى البيتِ، دون بيانات
تقطّعُ حلمي إلى جثثٍ ومخاوف
[أيها القلقُ المبتدا

أيها الوطنُ المنتهى
كلُّ ما نملكُ
وطنٌ مثل أحلامنا
وهوىً يهلكُ..........]
وأنا في عراءِ القذائفِ،
مَنْ أرتجي؟
رافعاً للسماءِ إنائي
أوزّعُ – بين ثقوبِ المواضع – وجهي
وهذا الفضاءَ القتيلْ

منكمشاً، مثل طيرٍ بليلْ
يمرُّ الرصاصُ الأخيرُ على جسدي
فيطرّزُ أيامَهُ بزهورِ الخراب
سأرتقُ في إبرِ الأمنياتِ
قميصَ شبابي الذي قُدَّ من جهةِ القلبِ
فتفتقُهُ الطلقاتُ
مَنْ يلمُّ الشظايا – غداً –
حينما تنتهي الحربُ، مرغمةً؟
مَنْ يعيدُ لأرملةِ الحربِ زهرَّها اليانعةْ؟
أتسلّلُ محترساً، تحتَ جنح الحنين
نحو غصنِ البلادِ الذي يتّفتقُ للتوِّ
أو يتيبّسُ للتوِّ
وأقارنُ بين غصونِ الربيع
وبين غصونِ القذيفة

22

A CLOUD OF GLUE

I proclaim: tomorrow
I will stretch across the broad light of day
Clouds will shade me and not war-planes
I will search among bombs and mud
For what is left of my life and my friends
I will fill my lungs with streets and jasmine
And set out for home without the communiqués of war
That chop up my dream into corpses and horrors
(O you first malaise
O you final homeland
    All that we own
            Is a country equal to our dreams
And an annihilating passion …)
And I amidst the nakedness of projectiles
Who will give me shelter?
Raising my canteen to the sky
I apportion – among the shattered bunkers –
My face and this murdered vastness,
Huddled like a drenched bird,
The last bullets passing over my body
Embroidering its days with flowers of destruction.
I will patch up, with needles of hope,
The shirt of my youth ripped over my heart
And the bullet holes will unravel my sewing
Who will gather up the shrapnel – tomorrow?
When the war is finally done with
Who will restore to the war widow her blossom?
Under the cover of nostalgia I steal away
Toward the branches of the country that have just been slashed
            Or have become desiccated
And I compare the branches in springtime
To the branches of the projectile

وأقولُ: صباحَ البلادِ
التي علمتنا التشتّتَ
بين كراسي المقاهي العتيقةِ، والاعترافِ المكهربِ
بين البيوتِ الخفيضةِ، والمرأةِ الغادرةْ
سوفَ تحشرنا في المواضعِ
ملتصقين، بصمغِ المخاوفِ ....
نرقبُ الأفقَ:
أسودَ.....
يخضرُّ بالأملِ — العشبِ، تحصدهُ الطائراتْ
أو أزرقاً....
سوف يحمرُّ من دمِنا
فتصادرهُ اللافتاتْ

أو رماداً بطيئاً

سيرسبُ في الروحِ
شيئاً، فشيئاً

كما الذكرياتْ

21/04/1987 النجف

هذا الألم.. الذي يضيء

ما أن أجلس على الكرسي – ذاتَ نهارٍ مشمسٍ –
صالباً ساقيَّ اللتين شوهتهما الحربُ
ومحدقاً في بريدِ الشوارعِ وهو يحملُ لي بطاقاتِ الأصدقاءِ المفقودةِ، والكسلَ،
والباصاتِ المسرعةَ، وغيومَ الدهشةِ..
مسترجعاً أمام عينيكِ السوداوين تأريخَ حزني الطويل

24

And I say: good morning, country!
    You taught us how to scatter
        Among old café chairs and chairs of torture
        Among decrepit houses, and deceitful women
We will be cramped up in bunkers
Stuck together with the glue of fear.
We are scanning the horizon:
        Black ...
        Greening, with hope – grass mown by planes
        Or blue ...
            Turning red with our blood
                And placards will sequester it
Or a slow ash
            Will settle on the soul
                Little by little

As our memories

Najaf (Iraq) 21/4/1987

THIS PAIN THAT SHINES

I'm just sitting here – on a sunny day –
My legs crossed, the ones buckled by war,
Folded in by the mail-storm of the street that will bring me
                postcards from lost friends, idleness,
Fast buses, clouds of unknowing,
Recounting for your melancholic eyes the long history of my
        sorrows,

وبمجردِ أن أرمشَ جفني
تتساقطُ صورُ القنابل بدل الدموع
كفاكِ تحديقاً في مرايا عيوني..
لقد بكيتُ كثيراً، أكثرَ مما يجبُ
أكثرَ من كميةِ الدموعِ المخصصةِ لحياتي

والآنْ..
عليَّ أن أبتسمَ أمامَ مرايا المطعم الفخمِ، الذي تطأهُ أقدامُ دهشتي لأولِ مرة،
محاطاً بذراعكِ نصفَ العارية
بينما يغطّي الفرو الثمينُ نصفَ العالم الشهي
اتركيني – لدقائق –
ريثما يهدأ هذا الهلعُ الذي يسكنني
منذ دخلتُ – سهواً – رصيدكِ العاطفي
اتركيني – لساعات –
ففي داخلي سنواتٌ من الوحلِ والهلعِ والرصاص
لن تمسحَها يافطةُ النادلِ الأجنبيِّ، وهو ينحني بأدبٍ جمٍّ،
ليزيل قطرات القهوة التي أسقطها ارتباكي
على قماشِ الطاولةِ الأبيض
كان عليّ – على الأقلِ – أن أحدثكِ قبل هذا
عن بساتين طفولتي التي حرثتها أسنانُ البلدوزرات والجنزرات

عن قلبي الذي ما زال يرتجفُ على الأرصفةِ، كلما مرَّ به ما يشبهُ شَعرها الطويل
عن القنابل التي حفرتْ ذكرياتِها على ملامحي
عن نساء الصالونات اللواتي تضاحكن لرؤية حذائي المغموسِ بالطين
عن الأرصفةِ التي شردتني في الأجازاتِ القصيرة [المسروقةِ]

26

When in the blink of an eyelid
Images of bombs start falling instead of tears
Enough of this gazing into my eyes …
I've already wept too much, more than I should,
More than the amount of tears allotted my life

And now …
I have to smile in front of the mirrors of this splendid restaurant
   that my astonished feet have just now walked me into
Folded in by your bare arms …
While precious wraps half-cover other alluring customers
Allow me – just a few moments –
While this anxiety inhabiting me subsides
Since I, accidentally, found the password to your tenderness
Allow me just a few hours to deal with
The years of mud and restlessness and bullets inside me
That the foreign waiter's cloth cannot remove – he's nudging me
   very politely
So he can wipe off the drops of coffee that in my confusion I spilt
Over the table's white cloth.
I should have told you, at the very least and before anything else,
About the gardens of my childhood ploughed up by the teeth of
   bulldozers and tanks,

About my heart that still trembles on pavements whenever it
   comes across anything that resembles her long hair,
About the bombs the memories of which are scarred into my face,
About the women of the salons who snigger at the sight of my
   mud-splattered boots,
About the pavements that banished me during my short times
   on leave (clandestine, stolen times)

والأشجار التي اختبأتْ في مساماتِ جلدي أثناء القصفِ
عن السنواتِ المرّة التي تركتْ طعمها عالقاً على شفتي..، حتى هذه اللحظة
من عصير أناناسكِ وفنجانِ قهوتي
كفاك تحديقاً في مرايا عيوني
أعرفُ.. أعرفُ.. أعرفُ
أعرفُ ذلك...
هذه الذكريات ضيّعتْ حياتي تماماً
أعرفُ، هذه القصائد التي غاصت معي في البرك،
وحملتها في الملاجيء والمقاهي والدروب
ستبقى معي أينما ارتحلتُ
أعرفُ، هذا القلب سيضيّعُ ما تبقى مني
لقد تورطتُ..
تورطتُ تماماً..
ورغم ذلك فلستُ على استعدادٍ
لأن أبدّلَ حياتي بأيةِ حياة على الاطلاقِ
فأنا أملكُ هذا الألمَ الذي يضيء

نهاية الثمانينات – بغداد

غياب

رسمَ بلاداً
على شرشفِ الطاولة
وملأها بالبيوتِ المضيئةِ والجسورِ والأشجارِ والقطط
قطعَ تذكرةً
وسافرَ إليها
محمّلاً بحقائبِه وأطفالِه

28

And the trees that hid in the pores of my skin during the
        bombardments,
About the bitter years the taste of which is still stuck to
        my lips even now,
Until this moment of your pineapple juice and my cup of coffee.
Enough of your staring into the mirrors of my eyes.
I know … I know … I know …
I know that …
These memories have ruined my life completely
I know that these poems that were mired with me in the swamps
And that I carried in bunkers, cafés and down narrow border tracks
Will stay with me wherever I go,
I know that this heart will squander whatever's left of me.
I'm already tangled up
Completely enmeshed …
And in spite of this I am not ready
To change my life for any other:
I am the owner of this pain that shines.

Baghdad late 1980s

ABSENCE

He drew a country
On the tablecloth
And filled it with lit-up houses, bridges, trees and cats
He purchased a ticket
And set off to go there
        taking his luggage and children with him

لكنَّ رجالَ الكمارك
أيقظوهُ عند الحدودِ
فرأى نادلَ البارِ
يهزُّهُ بعنف:
إلى أين تَهربُ بأحلامِكَ
ولمْ تدفعْ فاتورةَ الحسابْ

القاهرة 19/03/1990

تضيق البلاد

تضيقُ البلادُ
تضيقُ...
تضيقُ
وتتسعُ الورقةْ
البلادُ التي نصفُها حجرُ
والبلادُ التي دمعُها مطرْ
والبلادُ التي...
تبيعُ بنيها..
إذا جوّعتها الحروبُ
فماذا تبيعُ إذا جوّعتكَ البلادُ
وضاقتْ بدمعتكَ الحدقةْ
....
....
الجريدةُ منفاكَ
تصعدها سلماً، سلما

وتغادرها برما

But customs men
Woke him at the border.
It was then that he realised the bartender
Was shaking him roughly:
Where are you off to in your dreams
You with your bill not yet even paid.

Cairo 19/03/1990

THE COUNTRY SHRINKS

The country shrinks
shrinks ...
shrinks
and the pages expand.
The country, half of which is rock,
the country whose tears are rain,
the country whose ...
sells its sons
when wars starve them –
What will you sell when your country starves you
and your eyes cramp up with tears?
. . . .
. . . .
The newspaper's your exile
You climb it step by step

and leave it in boredom

تاركاً عند بابِ المحاسبِ أحلامَكَ النزقةْ
والقصيدةُ أبعد مما تصورتَ
أبعد...
أبعد...
يبتعدُ النخلُ والأهلُ
لا شيء غير رصيفِ التذكّرِ، مستوحشاً
وخطى روحكَ القلقةْ
كأنَّ السماءَ العريضةَ
أضيقُ من كوةٍ، في قطارِ الوداعِ الأخيرِ
وأنتَ تطلُ بدمعتكَ المطبقةْ
......
....
تضيقُ البيوتُ
وتتسعُ العائلةْ
تضيقُ النساءُ، الخنادقُ، والأصدقاءْ
وتتسعُ الطلقةُ القاتلةْ
وبينهما أنتَ مرتبكٌ ووحيدْ
بين أن تبتدي في شتاتِ الجنونْ
أو تنتهي في سباتِ السجونْ
مسافةُ كفين في سلسلةْ
بينهما يطفيءُ الحرسُ الواقفون سجائرهم
أنتَ لا تطلبُ المستحيلْ
وطناً للحنين
وتذكرةَ الحافلةْ

بغداد 1990

abandoning your wild dreams at the accountant's door.
The poem is further off than you had imagined,
further …
further …
Palm trees and family are far away,
nothing but the pavement of memories, alone,
and the strides of your troubled spirit
as if the wide-open sky
were narrower than the small window of the last farewell train,
And you looking out through your suppressed tears
……………
……………
The houses are shrinking
and the family expands
The women, the trenches, friends, all shrink,
and the killing shots increase
and you are among them, confused and lonely,
between beginning in a diaspora of madness
or ending in the torpor of prison,
the span of two shackled hands apart
between the idle guards stubbing out their cigarettes.
You are not asking for the impossible,
a homeland to long for,
a bus ticket to go.

Baghdad 1990

محاولة

ضعْهُ فوق السندانْ
واطرقْهُ بلا رحمْه
اطرْقهُ...
اطرْقهُ...
قلتُ له:
– اطرقْهُ بشدّة
اطرقْهُ يا حدادْ
اطرقْهُ...
كي يتمدّدَ
... هذا القلبُ
ويُصبحَ جسراً
يوصلني للنسيانْ

بغداد 10/06/1991

خرجتُ من الحربِ سهواً

أنا خارجٌ من زمانِ الخياناتِ
نحوَ البُكاءِ النبيل على {وطنٍ} أخضرٍ
حرثتهُ الخنازيرُ والسرفاتُ
أنا داخلٌ في مدارِ القصيدةِ
نصفَ طليقٍ
ونصفَ مصفّدْ
فعليكمْ رثائي بما تملكون من النادباتِ
وليسَ عليّ سوى أن أشيرَ لكمْ
بأصابعَ "نائلةٍ"
لقميصِ البلادِ المعلّقِ فوق رماحِ العشيرةِ
تنخبُهُ الطلقاتُ

34

ATTEMPT

Fix it on the anvil
And hammer it without mercy
Hit it …
Hammer it …
I told him:
Hammer it hard
Hammer it, blacksmith
So hard …
It will stretch
                this heart
And become a bridge
To carry me to oblivion

Baghdad 10/06/1991

I EMERGED FROM THE WAR UNAWARES

I emerged from the age of betrayals
Towards a noble weeping for a green homeland
Ploughed up by pigs and tank tracks
I entered the orbit of the poem
Half free
And half in shackles
So the lamentations are down to you and your hired mourners
And there is nothing for me to do but point out to you
With Na'ilah's fingers
The country's shirts slung across tribal spears
Perforated by gunshot

فينسالُ نهرُ الفراتِ المضرّجُ بين أصابعكم
حينما تكتبونْ
– عبثٌ كلُّ ما يكتبُ الشعراءُ

....

فهذا الزمانُ يعلّمنا
أن نصفّقَ للقاتلين
حينما يعبرون الرصيفَ إلى دمنا
وهذا الزمانُ يعلّمنا
أن نقصّرَ قاماتنا
.... كي تمرَّ الرياحُ على رسلها
أن نماشي القطيعَ إلى الكلأُ الموسميِّ

ولكنني..........
من خلال الحطام الذي خلّفتهُ المدافعُ
أرفعُ كفي معقَّرةً بالترابِ المدمّى.....
أمامَ عيونِ الزمانِ
أعلّمهُ كيفَ نحفرُ أسماءَنا بالأظافرِ
كي تتوهجَ: لا
نحنُ الذين خرجنا من الثكناتِ
نكشُّ ذبابَ العواصم عن جرحنا
أُخطيءُ – حين تمرُّ بنا الشاحناتُ الطويلةُ –
في عددِ الشهداءِ الذين مضوا في رحابِ القنابلْ
وفي عددِ الأصدقاءِ
الذين مضوا في الطوابير
لكني – والقصيدةُ { لم ترها بعدُ عينُ الرقابةِ } –
لا أُخطيءُ الوجعَ المر

حين نمرُّ على وجل الأمهاتِ
تسمّرنَ فوقَ رصيفِ المحطاتِ
يسألنَ مَنْ يعبرون إلى الحرب
أن يأخذوا ليلهنَّ الطويلَ
مناديلَ دمع تضمّدُ جرحَ المسافةِ

36

The Euphrates seeping bloodily through your fingers
As you write
– All that poets write is in vain
. . . .
For this age teaches us
To applaud the murderers
As they wade across the pavements of our blood
And this age teaches us
To diminish ourselves
so the winds may flow freely and keep
Pace with herds gone to summer pastures

But I …
From out of the wreckage the cannons left behind
Will raise my palm, covered with blood-drenched dust,
Before the eyes of the world.
I'll teach it how we finger-nail our names
So the word NO shines out
We who have come from the barracks
To shake metropolitan flies from our wounds
Can we be wrong – as such huge lorries pass us –
About the number of innocents gone off as bombs
And the number of friends
Queuing up to die
But I – the poem the censor's eye has not yet seen –
Am not mistaken about this bitter pain

When we get to the dread of mothers
Nailed down on railway platforms
Asking those going off to war
To take their night-long handkerchiefs
Of tears to heal the wound of distance

بين الرصاصةِ، والدعواتِ
يكابرنَ صبرَ السنينِ
أمامَ الأسرّةِ، فارغةٍ
في مستشفياتِ الحروبِ.. [... يشرّونَ فوقَ حبالِ الرياحِ
شراشفَ مَنْ رحلوا،
كي تجفّفها للذين سيأتون عما قليلٍ...]
....
إلى أين نمضي بأعمارنا – غضةً –
أيها الربُّ.........
سأكتمُ هذا الصراخَ بحنجرتي
ريثما تفطرونَ على صحفِ اليومِ، والشاي
أكتبُ عن قمرٍ سيجيءُ
وعن غيمةٍ عبرتْ قمحَنا
لتحطَّ على جرحِنا
أربّتُ فوق مواجعكمْ
كي أمرَّ كخيطِ القصيدةِ
يلظمُ قلبي بالطرقاتِ
أخيطُ قميصَ المنافي على قَدِّ أحزانكمْ
وأتركُ دمَّ قميصي الذي قُدَّ من قُبُلٍ
شاهدي ودليلي
لدى كاتبِ العدلِ
لمْ أُهزمْ....
أو أفرَّ – كخيلِ بني العمِّ –
من ساحةِ الحربِ
بيني وبين الرصاصِ مسافةُ صدقي
وهذي القصيدةُ، مبحوحةُ الصوتِ
من فرطِ ما هرولتْ في الخنادقِ
تصرخُ من فزعٍ وذهولٍ:
. أوقفوا قرعَ هَذي الطبولْ
مَنْ يمسحُ الآنَ عن قبوِ ذاكرتي
صورَ الأصدقاءِ الذين مضوا في بريدِ المعارك
بلا زهرةٍ أو نعاسٍ

Between the bullets and their prayers.
Patiently, they endure the years of
Facing vacant, empty beds
In field hospitals, hanging the shrouds of
The dead over wind-swept wash-ropes
So they'll be dry for those next in line.
. . . .
Where shall we take our lives – still so tender –
O Lord …
I will stifle this clamour in my throat
While you breakfast on tea and today's papers
I will write about a moon that is rising and
A cloud passing over our wheat-fields
To settle over our wounds.
I will soothe your sufferings
So I can move on like a line in a poem
Threading my heart through the alleyways.
I will sew a shirt of exile the size of your sorrows
And leave the blood of my slashed shirt
As my witness and evidence
Before the writer of justice.
I've not been defeated,
Nor have I fled – like my cousin's horses –
From the field of battle.
There is a distance of truth between me and the bullets
And this poem, its voice hoarse
From too much crawling through the trenches
and screaming out in terror and bewilderment:
Stop beating these drums
Who will delete from the labyrinths of my memory
Images of friends pronounced dead in dispatches
Leaving behind neither flower nor slumber

ولمْ يتركوا غيرَ عنوانٍ قلبي
أصدقائي الذين أضاعوا الطريقَ
إلى دمعِهمْ والمنازلْ
أصدقاءَ القنابلْ
أنا شخحتُ قبلَ أواني
ألمْ تبصروا رئتي سوّدتَها الشعاراتُ لا التبغُ
ألمْ تبصروا قامتي حدّبتها خطى العابرين إلى الأوسمةْ
آه... مما يكتّمُ قلبي...
وما تعلنُ الصحفُ والفتياتْ
[يراوغنَ نبضَ المحبِّ إلى مصعدِ الشقّةِ الفارهةْ]
سلاماً بلادَ السنابلْ
سلاماً بلادَ الجداولْ
سلاماً بلادي، التي كلما حاصرتَها القنابلْ
حملتْ جرحَها رايةً لتقاتلْ
ومالتْ على جهةِ الرومِ،
لا رومَ غيرَ الذي تركَ الأهلُ في ظهرنا
من طعانِ السنانِ المخاتلْ
....
....

على شفتي شجرٌ ذابلٌ، والفراتُ الذي مرَّ لمْ يرويني.
ورائي نباحُ الحروبِ العقيمةِ يطلقها الجنرالُ على
لحمنا، فنراوغُ أسنانَها والشظايا التي مشّطتْ شَعرَ
أطفالنا قبلَ أنْ يذهبوا للمدارسِ والـوردِ. أركضُ،
أركضُ، في غابةِ الموتِ، أجمعُ أحطابَ مَنْ رحلوا في
خريفِ المعاركِ، مرتقباً مثل نجمٍ حزينٍ، وقد خلّفوني
وحيداً هنا، لاقماً طرفَ دشداشتي وأراوغُ موتي بين
القنابلِ والشهداءِ. أنا شاعرٌ أكلتْ عمرَهُ الكلماتُ،
فكيفَ أرتّبُ هذي الحروفَ وأطلقها جملةً، دونَ أنْ
يزلقَ القلبُ – مرتبكاً – من لساني وينفجرُ اللغمُ،
أركضُ، أركضُ، قلبي على وطني: أينَ يدفنُ أبناءَهُ؟..
الأرضُ أصغرُ من
دمعِ أمي،

40

And nothing for an address but my heart
Friends who lost the way
To their grief, their homes,
Friends of the bombs
I have grown old
Before my time
Haven't you seen my lungs blackened by slogans?
Haven't you seen my body hunkering beneath medal-grabbers?
Oh! what does this heart hide …
What newspapers and loose women reveal
Duping lovers up lifts to fancy apartments
Greetings to the country of wheat
Greetings to the country of running waters
Greetings to my country, the one that, besieged by bombs,
Carried its wounds like a banner into battle
And rebelled against the authority of the Romans.
No Romans now but our own countrymen, ready
to back-stab us with their treacherous blades

. . . .
. . . .

A withered tree on my lips and the passing Euphrates has
not quenched my thirst. Behind me the barking of futile wars
unleashed on our flesh by the General, so that we'll have to
evade their teeth and the shrapnel that used to comb our children's hair before school and roses. I run, run through the for-
ests of death, gathering those gone in the autumn of battle as
kindling, on the look-out like a sad star, here alone, biting on
my *dishdasha*, dodging death between bombs and martyrs. I
am a poet whose life has been eaten by words, so how am I
to put these letters together to release a sentence, without my
heart slipping, bewildered, from my tongue causing a land-
mine to explode? I run, my heart on my motherland: Where
will she bury her sons? This earth, smaller than my mother's

أنفِضُ عن جلدِ طفلي الرصاصَ، فيجمعهُ في
إناءِ الطحينِ. تمرُّ الرياحُ بأوتارِ قلبي، فيصدحُ
حُزنُ المروجِ. يمرُّ الفراشُ على جرحنا، ويطيرُ
إلى الزهرِ. يا شجراً علّمتنا براعمُهُ أنْ نبرعمَ
غُصْنَ مواجعنا للربيع الذي سوفَ يأتي لكي
يفتح الياسمينُ نوافذَهُ. آه لو يعقلُ الياسمينُ
وقلبي! تلوذُ بمعطفهِ – إذْ تمرُّ بها الطائراتُ –
ترى نبضَهُ دافقاً كالحديقةِ، ملتصقاً بالتُوّيجِ
الـذي كـانَ يرعشُ تحتَ القميص البليلِ:
أحبِّ.....كِ..!.. تقطعها الصافراتُ، فتنفرطُ
القُبلاتُ على العُشْبِ، تحرثُها السُرفاتُ إلى
آخرِ الياسمينِ وحُزني. تُعَلِّقُ ما ظلَّ من زعلٍ
فوق شَمّاعةِ الحـربِ، ينحدرُ الليلُ صوبَ
المنازلِ، وادعة في مساءِ التشابهِ والزنبق المرِّ،
ينحدرُ الطيرُ نحو سقوفِ المخازنِ، يهرعُ
سِرْبُ الكراكي إلى نبع روحي. غداً في صباحٍ
بلا طائراتٍ سنركضُ تحتَ رَذاذِ البنفسجِ،
ملتصقَين،.. نلفُّ الـشـوارعَ والكركراتِ،
نمسّدُ شَعرَ النوافيرِ. أذكرُ أنَّ يديكِ تحبّان أنْ
تنعسا في يديَّ، ونَكْبُرَ، هل يَكْبُرُ الحقلُ من
زهرةٍ،.. أم يديكِ؟ أرى ما أرى من جنونٍ
الحياةَ على صدرها، هائم الروح كالقبّراتِ،
ألمّ الأزاهيرَ عن ثوبِها والمروجَ التي حصدتْها
الشظايا. يتعتعني عسلٌ سـالَ مـن خطأ
الشفتين، – أأخطأتُ في الحبِّ!؟ أنَّ الممرَّ
الذي ضمّنا تحتَ ظلٍّ الصنوبرِ يذكرُ كيفَ
تسلَّلَ قلبي لصدركِ في غفلةٍ من يديَّ،...
– أأفرطتُ في الشربِ!؟ – لا توهميني بأنَّكِ
أكثر دفئاً من الأرضِ، هذي البلادُ على بُعْدِ
قنبلةٍ من وريدكَ يا أيُّها الطائرُ المتغرّبُ بين
القواميسِ. إنّا نقيسُ الحياةَ على حجمِ قنبلةٍ،
عَبَرَتْ صبرَنا الصعبَ،

tears. I'll shake the bullets off my son's skin and he will gather them in the flour bin. Winds pass through my heart-strings, and sorrow sings in the meadow. Butter-flies fly over our wounds, then on toward flowers. You trees, whose buds have taught us to sprout branches from our suffering that spring might come and jasmine open its windows. If only the jasmine and my heart would be reasonable! She takes refuge in his coat as war planes fly over, feels his pulse spring-bursting like the garden, brushing the corolla beneath her wet shirt. I lo-ve ... yo-u! Sirens pull her away and kisses are scattered on the grass, earthworms plough them down deep to jasmine and heart-sorrow. We hang what is left of anger on the hook of war, night descends on the houses, peaceful in the vagueness of evening and bitter lilies, birds descend over warehouse roofs, a flight of cranes wheels into my soul's spring. Tomorrow in a dawn without war planes, we'll run under drizzling violets, we'll melt together ... we'll wander through streets of laughter, we'll stroke the fountain's hair. I'll remember how your hands loved to slumber in my hands, and we will grow – does the field grow from a flower or from your hands? I will see what I see of love's madness on her breast, my soul carried off like a lark, I will gather flowers from her dress and from meadows mowed by shrapnel. Honey pouring from the lips' error make me stagger ... is that love's effect? The path that brought us together in the pine trees' shade remem-bers how my heart stole off to your breast without my hands noticing ... had I drunk too much? Don't convince me you're warmer than the land, this country is at a bomb's distance from your veins and you a migrant bird among dictionaries. We measure life with the calibre of a grenade, as it arcs across our long-suffered patience, we'll subtract it from the excess of

نسقطُ منها الشظايا – الزوائدَ، كي نرتديها، قميصاً من البهجةِ المستحيلةِ،

هلْ

خطأٌ

أنْ

نحبَّ

الحياةُ!؟...

14/12/1991 بغداد

سذاجة

كلما سقطَ دكتاتور
من عرشِ التاريخ، المرصّع بدموعنا
التهبتْ كفاي بالتصفيق
لكنني حالما أعود الى البيتِ
وأضغطُ على زرِ التلفزيون
يندلقُ دكتاتورٌ آخر
من أفواهِ الجماهيرِ الملتهبةِ بالصفيرِ والهتافات
.. غارقاً في الضحكِ
من سذاجتي
التهبتْ عيناي بالدموع

29/06/1992 بغداد – حدائق جمعية المؤرخين

44

shrapnel and wear it like a shirt of impossible, absurd joy, so
        is it
            wrong
                that we
                    so love
                        Life !? …

Baghdad 14/12/1991

GULLIBILITY

Whenever a dictator was toppled
From the tear-soaked throne of history,
My palms blazed up from the applause
But as soon as I get back home
And switch on the television
Another dictator gushes out
Of the mouths of the crowd on fire with adulation
… I drown in laughter
        at my gullibility
My eyes burning with tears

Baghdad 29/06/1992

شهداء الانتفاضة

هؤلاء الذين
تساقطوا أكداساً
أمامَ دباباتِ الحرس
هؤلاء الذين حلموا كثيراً بالأرض
قبل أن يحلّقوا بأجنحتهم البيضاء
هؤلاء الذين نما على شواهدِ قبورهم صبّيرُ النسيان
هؤلاء الذين تآكلتْ أخبارُهم
شيئاً ، فشيئاً..
في زحمة المدينة
إنّهم يتطلعون بعيونٍ مشدوهةٍ
إلى قدرتنا على نسيانهم بهذهِ السرعة

بغداد 1992

ثقب

طلقةٌ عابرةٌ
ثقبتْ نومَهُ
فتدفقَ
– فوق وسادتِهِ –
لزجاً
دمُ أحلامِهِ الخاسرةُ

بغداد 01/01/1993

46

MARTYRS OF THE UPRISING

Those who
were heaped in piles
before the tanks of the Guard,
those who so often dreamed of land
and then flew off with white wings,
those whose tombstones fertilised cacti of oblivion
those whose stories were eroded …
piece by piece
                    in the city's tumult
see how they look, astonished
at our ability to forget them
so absolutely

Baghdad 1992

A HOLE

A glancing shot
punctured his sleep
and the blood of
defeated dreams
gushed viscous
onto his pillow.

Baghdad 01/01/1993

47

أجاممنون

عائداً...
من غبارِ الحربِ
بقلبٍ مجرّح
وذراعين من طبولٍ وذهب
حالماً بشفتي كليتمنسترا، العسليتين
اللتين كانتا في تلك اللحظة
تذوبان على شفتي عشيقها ايجستوس   ليلةً، ليلة
عندما فتحَ البابَ
رأى في دبقِ شفتيها
الآفَ الجثثِ التي تركها في العراء

فتذكر
أنه نسي أن يتركَ جثتَهُ هناك .

14/01/1993 بغداد

في حديقة الجندي المجهول

الجندي، الذي نسي أن يحلقَ ذقنَهُ
ذلكَ الصباح
فعاقبهُ العريف
الجندي القتيلُ، الذي نسوه في غبارِ الميدان
الجندي الحالمُ، بلحيتِهِ الكثّة
التي أخذتْ تنمو
شيئاً، فشيئاً
حتى أصبحتْ . بعد عشر سنوات .
غابةً متشابكةَ الأغصانْ

48

AGAMEMNON

He came back
from the dust of war
with a wounded heart, his
arms full with drums and gold
dreaming of Clytemnestra's
honeyed lips that at that very
moment Aegisthus was melting
with his own, as every night.
And as he opened the door
he sensed on her lips' grease
the thousands of corpses he'd
abandoned under the open sky
and recalled how he'd forgotten
to leave his own body there.

Baghdad 14/01/1993

IN THE GARDEN OF THE UNKNOWN SOLDIER

The soldier who that morning forgot
                    to shave his hair
and was punished for it by his Sergeant,
the soldier left fallen in the dust of battle,
the dreaming soldier, with his thick beard
                    that got to grow
                    little by little
until, after ten years, it was a forest
                    of tangled bush,

تصدحُ فيها البلابلْ
ويلهو في أراجيحها الصبيانْ
ويتعانقُ تحت أفيائها العشاقْ
....
....
الجندي..
الذي غدا متنزهاً للمدينة
ماذا لو كان قد حلقَ ذقنَهُ، ذلك الصباح

28/09/1993 عمان

مفتتح

أتصفّحُ كتبَ التاريخ
فتتلوّثُ أصابعي...
... بالدم
كلما قلبتُ فصلاً لطاغية
قادني حرّاسُهُ
إلى الفهرست
فأرتجف هلعاً
أيها الجنرالات
ماذا صنعتم بأحلامنا؟
أكلُّ هذه الجزماتِ السودِ
التي تسلّقتْ أعناقَنا
وما زلنا نلوّحُ للشمس!؟

10/11/1993 عدن

50

such that nightingales sang in its branches
and children always played on its swings
and lovers came closer in its shade
. . . .
. . . .
That soldier
who grew into a park for the whole town,
        what if that day he'd shaved his head?

Amman 28/09/1993

GAMBIT

I thumb the history books
And my fingers get soiled …
                … with blood
Whenever I get to a new chapter regarding a tyrant
His guards lead me
To the index
And I quake with fear
    Generals!
        What have you done to our dreams?
All these black boots
That have clambered rough-shod over our necks
And yet we still keep saluting the sun!

Aden 10/11/1993

ما حدث للحكيم

بينما كان يلقي محاضرتَهُ..
في القاعةِ المحتشدةِ
كانوا هناك
يفصّلون جثتَهُ على مقاسِ التقاريرِ الواردةِ
ويتركون ما تبقى من دمِهِ
في ثلاجةِ العائلة
حين ترجّلَ من المنصّةِ
وسطَ موسيقى التصفيق
تحسّسَ عنقه
لمْ يجدْ غيرَ فراغٍ مهولٍ
وثمّةَ حزٌّ طويلٌ، ما زال نديّاً فوق ياقتهِ
ركضَ هلعاً إلى الجمهور...
مستنجداً بالكراسي... الفارغة
متعثّراً بقهقهات الصدى
....
....
لا أحد،
غير حارسٍ عجوزٍ
كان يهذي
عن رجلٍ مخبولٍ
شاهده — قبل قليل —
يبحثُ...
بين المقاعدِ
عن رأسِه المقطوع

1993 عمّان

WHAT HAPPENED TO THE SAGE

As he was delivering his talk
to the crowded hall
They were there
dissecting his corpse according to
the pattern of intelligence reports
leaving the remains of his blood
in the family fridge.
When he came down off the podium
amid the music of applause
he felt for his neck
found nothing but a dreadful void
and a deep gash, damp across his collar.
He ran in panic into the audience
craving the safety of the empty chairs
stumbling over the echoes' guffaws
. . . .
. . . .
Nobody
just an old attendant
drivelling on about
some mad man
he'd seen a moment before –
with his own eyes –
searching between the seats
for his severed head

Amman 1993

53

منتهى

أفتحُ ثلاجةَ أحزاني
أخرجُ قنينةَ عرق
وأشربها كلها
نخبَ أصدقائي المهاجرين
عبرَ الأنفاقِ
بلا وطن
ولا سجائر
ولا جوازات سفر
أرفعُ أنخابَهم كأساً، كأساً
أو جثةً، جثةً
وحين أسقطُ على الرصيفِ
من الثمالة
سيحملونني — في توابيتهم —
إلى البيت

23/05/1993 بغداد

تحت سماء غريبة

معادلةٌ صعبةٌ
أن توزّعَ نفسكَ بين فتاتين
بين بلادين
من حرسٍ وأناناس
بينهما، أنتَ ملتصقٌ بالزجاجةِ
في حانةٍ، تتقافزُ فيها الصراصيرُ
كانتْ لكَ الكلماتُ، الطريقَ إلى النخلِ..
من أين جاؤوا بأسوارهم
فانتحيتَ، تراقبُ

54

END

From the icebox of
sadness, I take out the arak
and drink the whole bottle.
I drink to my friends, all exiles,
through the tunnels
            without country, without
            cigarettes, without passports
I raise a toast, glass after glass,
then corpse after corpse.
And when I collapse on the street
from my drunkenness
it is they who will carry me
home in their coffins.

Baghdad 1993

UNDER A STRANGE SKY

A difficult balance
dividing yourself between two women
            two countries
            of police and pineapples, date-palms and data
Between the two you cling to a bottle
    in a tavern crawling with cockroaches
Once you had the words and path to the palm trees
Where did they come from with their walls?
You turned aside to look at

ضوءَ الصواري البعيدةِ
يخبو ، ويصعدُ
بين الشهيقِ، وبين الزفير

....

....

معادلةٌ مرَّةٌ
أن تظلَّ كما أنتَ
ملقىً على الرملِ
ترسمُ أفقاً، وتمحوهُ
برقاً، وتجلوهُ
إنَّ السماءَ القريبةَ، أشهى
السماءَ البعيدةَ.. أبهى
لكن أحذية الحرس الملكيِّ
ستحجبُ عنك فضاءَ الحنينِ المعرَّش
ما بين أزهارِ قلبكَ، والنافذة

....

....

معادلةٌ صعبةٌ
أن أبدّلَ حلماً، بوهمٍ
وأنثى،.. بأخرى

ومنفىً، بمنفى
وأسألُ:
أين الطريق!؟

11/01/1994 عمان

56

       the light of distant masts
    rising and falling
    between out-breath and in
....
....
A bitter balance
to remain as you are
   tossed on the sands
outlining a horizon, then wiping it away
      A flash of lightning and removing it
the sky nearby more agreeable
      the distant sky ... more radiant
But the boots of the royal guard
   will bar you from the zone of nostalgias that
      twine between the blossoms of your heart and the window
....
....

A difficult balance
exchanging a dream for an illusion
    one woman for another

    an exile for an exile
And I say to you,
    where is the path?

Amman 11/01/1994

شكوى

نَظَرَ الأعرجُ إلى السماء
وهتفَ بغضبٍ:
أيها الربُّ
إذا لمْ يكنْ لديكَ طينٌ كافٍ
فعلامَ تعجّلتَ في تكويني

1994 عمان

تشكيل

أرسمُ دبابةً وأوجهها إلى شرفةِ الجنرال
أرسمُ غيمةً وأقولُ: تلك بلادي
أرسمُ لغماً وأضعهُ في خزانةِ اللغة
أرسمُ عنكبوتاً وأحطّطهُ على بابِ الأحزان
أرسمُ أبي وأقولُ له: لماذا تركتني وحيداً أمام اللئام
أرسمُ مائدةً وأدعو إليها طفولتي
أرسمُ ناياً وأنسلُ من ثقوبهِ إلى القرى البعيدة
أرسمُ شارعاً وأتسكعُ فيه مع أحلامي
أرسمُ قلبي...
... واسأله: أين أنتِ!؟

27/12/1995

COMPLAINT

A lame man looked at the sky
And cried out in anger:
O Lord
If you hadn't enough clay
Why the haste to create me?

Amman 1994

DRAWING

I fashion a tank and point it towards the General's balcony
I fashion a cloud and say, this is my country
I fashion a land mine and place it in the cupboard of words
I fashion a spider and am embalmed on the doorway of sorrows
I fashion my father and tell him: why did you abandon me
       to the wicked?
I fashion a table and invite my childhood days to sit there
I fashion a flute and slip through its stops to remote villages
I fashion a street and wander in it together with my dreams
I fashion my heart …
       and ask it where you are?

27/12/1995

تأويل

يملوني سطوراً
ويبوبونني فصولاً
ثم يفهرسونني
ويطبعونني كاملاً
ويوزعونني على المكتباتِ
ويشتمونني في الجرائدِ
وأنا
لمْ
أفتحْ
فمي
بعد

1996 دمشق

حساب

أيها الربُّ
افرشْ دفاترك
وسأفرش أمعائي
وتعال نتحاسبْ

1996 بيروت

60

CRITICAL

They write up my lines
split me into chapters
catalogue my references
print the whole works
get me in the bookshops
bad-mouth me in print
and I
haven't
even
opened my
mouth:
yet!

Damascus 1996

RECKONING

O Lord
Spread out Your records
And I will spill my intestines
Then let's settle our scores

Beirut 1996

الحلاج

أصعدني الحلاجُ إلى أعلى تلٍّ
في بغداد
وأراني كلَّ مآذنها
ومعابدها
وكنائسها ذات الأجراسْ
وأشار إليَّ:
– أحصِ
كم دعواتٍ حرّى تتصاعد يومياً من أنفاسِ الناسْ
لكنْ لا أحدَ
حاولَ أن يصعدَ
في معناهُ إلى رؤياهُ
ليريهِ..
ما عاثَ طغاةُ الأرضِ
وما اشتطَّ الفقهاءُ
وما فعلَ الحراسْ

بيروت 10/08/1996

62

AL-HALLAJ*

Al-Hallaj took me
To the highest hill in Baghdad
And showed me all its
Minarets and temples,
Churches and bells
Then he beckoned me.
'Look', he said, 'count
How many prayers daily rise up
From our breaths, yet no-one
Ever tries to ascend
From His meaning to His vision
So as to warn Him of
The ravages of all the tyrants
The deviations of the jurists
And what the guards have done.'

Beirut 10/08/1996

* A legendary Sufi master who lived between 858-922 AD and inspired
many subsequent Sufi mystics, including Rumi. He was tortured
and publicly executed by the Abbasid rulers for what they deemed
"theological error" threatening the security of the state.

نقود الله

على رصيفِ شارع الحمراء
يعبرُ رجلُ الدين بِمَسبحتِهِ الطويلةِ
يعبرُ الصعلوكُ بأحلامِهِ الحافيةِ
يعبرُ السياسي مفتّخاً برأسِ المالِ
يعبرُ المثقف ضائعاً
بين سوهو وحي السلّم
الكلُّ يمرُّ مسرعاً ولا يلتفتُ
للمتسولِ الأعمى
وحدهُ المطرُ ينقّطُ على راحتِهِ الممدودةِ
باتجاهِ الله

1996 مقهى الكوبي دو باغيه – بيروت

مقاطع من "نشيد أوروك"

من تحت أنقاضِ عصرِ الطواغيتِ،
ينهضُ قلبي
يغني.........
لعاشقةٍ، رحلَتْ كذبولِ قرنفلةٍ
فوق شطآنِ اينون*
فانتحبَ الكورسُ:
أنساكَ شهدُ اللذاذاتِ، سهدَ التجاريبِ
لكن روحيَ شوّهها السجنُ
....
...

*– بحيرة صغيرة في سومر.

64

GOD'S MONEY

On al-Hamra' street
The religious man walks with his rosary
The tramp goes by with barefoot dreams
The politician crosses, wasted with gain
The intellectual passes, vaguely astray
Between Soho and Hay al-Sillem.
All rush past, sparing not a thought
For the blind beggar
Only rain drips onto his palms
Stretching out to God

Café de Baquet, Beirut 1996

from 'URUK'S ANTHEM'

From beneath the rubble of the age of tyrants ,
        my heart shall rise
                singing …
        to a lover, a faded carnation
    on Enon's* shore,
The chorus thus lamenting:
The honeys of pleasure have made you forget the insomnia
    of ordeals
but prison has distorted my soul
……………
…

* Enon is a small lake in Sumar, a district in Iraq

قلتُ: اتركوني، لأنشقَ رائحةَ اللوزِ في فمها..
هاهي آثارهم تحفرُ القلبَ لا الجلدَ
مرحى لهُ كلما عبرتْ طلقةٌ، ينحني كي يلملمَ ما قد تدحرجَ من نبضهِ في بلاطِ
الرصيفِ، تشاهدهُ امرأةٌ من سياجِ الحديقةِ، تصرخُ مذعورةٌ:
احذرِ المركباتِ السريعةَ،
أنَّ جلالَتَهُ يمرقُ الآن.....

لكنهم حملوهُ بعيداً...
وتذكرُ زوجتهُ – وجنتاها مآتمُ منصوبةٌ – أنهم فتشوا البيتَ،
حتى دفاترِ طفلتها المدرسية،
ثم رموهُ على باهم
كالبصاقِ

وتذكرُ – بعد سنينٍ – بأنَّ الطبيبَ الذي جسَّ شريانَهُ، كان يسمعُ في دمِهِ،
دفقَ الحشدِ،
يهتفُ:
– "عاااااااااااااااااااااااااااااشَ".....
تصعدهُ الطلقاتُ البعيدةُ
لكنها انتبهتْ – في مساءٍ حزين –
لصوتِ أنينٍ يدحرجُ فوق الوسادةِ أنفاسَهُ ثم يسقطُ...
تهمسُ:
هل قلتَ: يسـقطُ؟!!
!!!..

ينهضُ مرتعباً،
يتعوذُ مما يُدسُّ بأحلامِهِ،
ثم يلبسُ أثوابَهُ عجلاً

I said: let me smell the fragrance of almonds in her mouth
Look, their traces have carved out the heart not the skin
Glory be to every passing bullet, he leans
down to gather up whatever might have rolled from his
          heartbeat onto the paving stones,
A woman is watching him from her garden fence, she shouts
          in panic,
    'Mind out for the speeding cars,
    His Majesty's heading this way right now ...'

Even so they took him off far away ...
And his wife remembers – her cheeks distraught mourners
    – how they searched the house, even her daughter's
          school notebooks,
Then they flung him into the doorway
          Like spat spittle

And she remembers – years later – that the doctor who was
          taking his pulse could hear in his blood the flowing
                multitudes, their screaming
– *Vi-i-i-i-i-i-VA* ...
The distant shots amplifying it.
Yet she was woken, on a sad evening,
by a plaintive moan rolling his breath over the pillow and
          then falling ...
She whispers,
'Did you say 'Falling?
... !!!'

He gets up terrified
seeking refuge from that which is buried deep in his dreams,
          then puts his clothes on hastily

ليسلمهم رأسَهُ:

- سيدي، كان هذا يغافلني
- في الليالي —
ويشتمكم....

....
....

مرحى، لكم دورةُ الأرضِ
لي، دورةُ الحبرِ
مرحى، لمن حقنوهُ بمصلِ المعاشِ،
فعاشَ،
ليهتف:
"عااااشَ"،
لمن ينصبون فخاخَ الشعاراتِ،
نلصقها
ثم نسقطُ...
كي يصعدَ الجنرالُ إلى بجدهِ،
جثةً، جثةً
ويحيي الجموعَ التي أجّلتْ موتها
كي تصفّقَ.....

. . . .

. . . .

....
....
- كمْ ساعتكَ الآنَ؟
- منتصفَ الموتِ، ببغداد.........
ورجالُ الآر بي جي خلفَ النخلِ يدكّون قلاعَ الدكتاتورِ (يفتّشُ بين الأدراجِ عن
الحرس الخاص:
لقد فروا) فيلوذُ بزاويةِ المرحاضِ..
يموتُ وحيداً مذعوراً..
يسحلهُ صرصارٌ من ياقتهِ،
- بين الأنقاضِ -

68

in order to deliver his head to them:
'Sir, this head, it's been catching me unawares
            in the night
                and vilifying you'

. . . .
. . . .

Bravo, for the turning of the Earth
for me, the rotation of ink
Bravo for the one they injected with life's serum
so he can live on
to shout out
            Vi-i-i-i-i-i-VA,
For the one who sets up the traps of the slogans
            we glue them up
and then down we fall down
that the General may ascend to his glory,
corpse by corpse
and stage-manage the masses whose death has been postponed
            that they might keep on with their clapping

. . . .
. . . .

                        ૭

. . . .
. . . .

– What time is it now?
– Half-past death, Baghdad time …
And the RBG men behind the palm trees are razing the
            dictator's strongholds to the ground (he's looking on
            the stairs for his personal guard; they've fled) so he
            takes refuge in the corner by the latrine
He's dying, alone and terrified …
A cockroach drags him along by the collar,
                amidst the rubble,

يُخشخشُ بالأوسمةِ الذهبيةِ
تعترِكُ الديدانُ على جثتِه
كاميراتُ الصحفيين
تعلّقه – فوق الجسرِ –
أكفُّ الشعبِ الهادرِ
لافتةً
لنهايةِ عصرِ الطغيانْ

....

....

قلتُ: انتظرتكَ.......
نمضي معاً في الأزقةِ (لا بيتَ لي
غير ظلِّ القصيدةِ
أفرشهُ وأنامُ)

شريدين،
تنكرنا واجهاتُ الفنادقِ
والطرقاتُ الغريبةُ
متكئاً فوق كتفي،
يبلّلُ دمعُكَ عشبَ قميصي

فتمسحُ عن مقلتي
نثارَ النجومِ..
ونحلمُ....
نحلمُ ...
نحلمُ

[كلٌّ يغني على ليلهِ....
وأنا في مديريةِ الأمنِ كنتُ أغني على كلِّ ما مرَّ..]
حتى إذا أورقَ الفجرُ
– فوق غصونِ المصاطبِ –

70

His gold medals clinking
They fight over his corpse, the worms and
  the journalists' cameras.
  They hang him over the bridge
the hands of the roaring crowds
  as a banner
    for the end of the age of oppression
....
....

I said 'I waited for you ... '
That we should go together through the alleyways
    (I have no home but the poem's shadow,
      I spread it out and sleep)
Vagabonds,
  the hotels' facades ignore us
    and the foreign roads
leaning on my shoulder,
  your tears wet the grass of my shirt

        ॐ

Then you wipe from your eyes
    the dust of the stars
     and we dream ...
      we dream ...
       we dream ...

(Everyone sings in their dark hours ...
And I was singing in the prison block for all that was gone)
Until dawn puts forth leaves
on the branches of the benches

ودعتني....
    ومضيتَ وحيداً
        لمنفاكَ
تنشدُ في الريحِ منكسراً
    مثلَ نايٍّ غريبٍ:

      – أماناً
      بلادي
      التي
      لن
      أ
      ر
      ى....
      ....
      ....

1996-1984

المحذوف من رسالة الغفران

مستلقياً على ظهري
أحدّقُ في السماءِ الزرقاء
وأحصي كمْ عددَ الزفراتِ التي تصعدُ إلى اللهِ كلَّ يومٍ
وكم عددَ حبات المطر التي تتساقطُ من جفنيهِ
أديرُ قرصَ الهاتفِ

You bade me farewell …
	and went off alone
	to your exile
Singing, shattered in the wind
		like a strange flute

– Peace to
my country
which I
will never

s
	e
		e
. . . .
. . . .

	1984-1996

DELETED PART OF 'RISALAT AL-GHUFRAN'*

Lying on my back
and looking up at the sky
I count the sighs rising up to God each day
and the drops of rain dripping from His eyelids
and I call Him on the phone and

* Famous book by the rebellious blind poet Abul Ala'a al-Ma'ari (973-
1057 AD). Its sceptical humanism and brilliant language is said to
have been an inspiration for Dante's *Divine Comedy*.

73

وأطلبهُ
ترُدُّ سكرتيرتهُ الجميلةُ
إنه مشغول هذه الأيام
إلى أذنيهِ
بتقليبِ عرائضكم التي تهرأتْ من طولِ تململها في المخازن
يا سيدتي أريدُ رؤيتَهُ ولو لدقيقةٍ واحدةٍ

ما مِنْ مرة
طلبتهُ
وردَّ عليَّ
أريدُ أنْ أسألَهُ قبلَ أنْ أودّعَ حياتي البائسة
وقبل أنْ يضعَ فواتيرَهُ الطويلةَ أمامي:
يا إلهي العادل
أمِن أجلِ تفاحةٍ واحدةٍ
خسرتُ جنانَكَ الواسعةَ
أمِن أجلِ أن يسجدَ لي ملاكٌ واحدٌ
لم يبقَ شيءٌ في التاريخ إلا وركعتُ أمامه
....

يا أبانا...
يا أبانا الرحيم
أعرف أنكَ لنْ تضحكَ على ذقوننا مثلهم
لكني مهانٌ ويائس

أريدُ شبراً من هذه الأرض الواسعةِ أضعُ عليه رأسي ونعالي وأنام
أريد رغيفاً واحداً من ملايين السنابل التي تتمايس أمامي كخصورِ الراقصات
....
......
أجلسُ أمامَ بابِ مسجدِ الكوفة
أجلسُ أمامَ كنيسةِ لوند
أجلسُ أمامَ حائطِ المبكى

ask for Him.
His pretty secretary replies
that these days He's so busy
so snowed under
with all our tattered petitions stacked in the store rooms.
My dear lady, I mouth at her, I so need to see Him
if only for one moment,
but He's never replied
whatever I've asked.
I want to appeal to Him before I take leave of my miserable life
and before He lays before me the inventory of my sins.

My God, the Most Just,
did I lose such a vast paradise
simply on account of one apple?
Was it because of but one fallen angel
that I had so to prostrate myself in humiliation?
. . . .
Our Father ...
Our Father most Merciful
I know You won't make fun of me as they do
but I feel miserable and without hope

I simply want a patch of this earth to lay me down, shoeless,
        to sleep
just one loaf of bread from among the teeming ears of wheat
that sway before me like dancers' waists
. . . .
. . . .
I sit in front of the door of the Kufa Mosque
I sit in front of the Cathedral of Lund
I sit in front of the Wailing Wall

أجلسُ أمامَ معبدِ بوذا
ضاغطاً راحتي على رَكبتي
وأحصي كمْ يصعدون، ظهورَنا المحدودبةَ كالسلالم
وكم ينزِلُون
ومع هذا
لا أحد يلتفتُ إلى دموعنا المنسابةِ كالمزاريب

أريدُ أن أصعدَ يوماً إلى ملكوته
لأرى..
إلى أين تذهبُ غيومُ حشرجاتنا
وهذه الأرض التي تدور
بمعاركنا وطبولنا وشتائمنا واستغاثاتنا
منذ ملايين السنين
ألمْ توقظْهُ من قيلولتِهِ الكونيةِ
ليطلَّ من شرفتِهِ
وينظر لنا
مَنْ يدري
ربما سئمَ من شكوانا
فأشاحَ بوجههِ الكريم
ونسينا إلى الأبد.
أحلمُ أن أركلَ الكرةَ الأرضيةَ بحذائي المثقوب
ولا أدعها تسقطُ
حتى أعيدها إليه
كي يجيبني
بعيداً عن جمهرةِ المفسرين والدراويش والوعّاظ:
إذا كنتَ وحدكَ مالكَ الغيب..
ولمْ تفشِ أسرارَكَ لأحدٍ
فكيف علمَ أبليس
بأني سأعيثُ في الأرضِ فساداً
....
وإذ كنتَ حرمتني
من دم العنقودِ
فلماذا أبحتهُ لغيري

76

I sit in front of the temple of Buddha
my hand palm-pressed to my knee
and I see how many times we've raised our hunched backs
and how many times we've bowed ourselves down
and in spite of all this
no-one pays any attention to our guttered gush of tears

Ah, I want to go to His Kingdom one day to see
where the clouds of our moaning end up,
and this planet that has been rotating
with our scuffles and drums, our curses and supplications
down so many millions of years
as to wake Him from His cosmic siesta
that He might look out from His balcony
and observe us.
And who knows,
maybe He's become bored with our grievances
and has turned His Holy Face away
and forgotten us forever.
It seems I'm kicking the terrestrial globe with pokey shoes
and that I'm not letting it hit the ground
until I can pass it back to Him
And then He can reply to me
out of sight of the exegetes and dervishes and preachers.
If You and only You were master of the hidden
and disclosed not Your secrets to anyone,
then how did Satan come to know
that I'd wreak havoc on this planet
. . . .
And if You denied me
the blood of grapes
then why did You allow it to others?

....
وإذا كان الأشرارُ لمْ يصعدوا إلى سفينةِ نوح
وغرقوا في البحرِ
فكيفَ امتلأتِ الأرضُ بهم ثانيةً
....
و "إذا السماء انشقّتْ، وأذِنتْ لربها وحُقّتْ، وإذا الأرضُ مُدّتْ، وألقتْ ما فيها
وتخلّتْ".
فأين ستذهب لوحات فان كوخ،
وقصائد المتنبي،
ومسرحيات شكسبير،
ونهج البلاغة،
وسمفونيات موزارت

وما الذي سنجده في متاحفِ الجنة..
....

وإذا كنتُ سأجدُ في فراديسك الواسعة
حبراً
وخمراً
وصفصافاً
فهل أستطيعُ نشرَ قصائدي
دونَ أن تمرَّ على رقيبٍ
....
وإذا أنكحتني
عشرةَ آلافِ حورية عينٍ...
فماذا ستترك لحبيبتي
و......
و..........

03/04/1997 لوليو- جنوب القطب الشمالي

78

. . . .
And if the wicked could not get on board Noah's Ark
but were instead drowned in the seas
how are they come back to this Earth again?
. . . .
"When heaven shall be split asunder, and listen to and obey
   its Lord, as it must, and when the earth shall be stretched
   out and shall cast forth all that was in it and be empty..."*
What will happen to Van Gogh's paintings,
      and al-Mutanabbi's qasidas,
         and Shakespeare's plays,
            and the *Nahj al-Balagha***,
               and Mozart's music?
And what will be left us in the museums of Paradise?
. . . .

And if in Your vast Paradise I could find
ink and
wine and
         reed-pens
then might I publish my poems
without need of the censor?
. . . .
And if You were to give me
ten thousand *houris* to dandle
what would be left for my Love?
And ...
And ...

   Luleå, Sweden 03/04/1997

* Verses 1-4, Sura 84 (The Splitting Asunder), *The Qur'an*
** *Nahj al-Balagha* is the most famous collection of speeches attributed
to Imam Ali Ibn Talib, the cousin of the Prophet Muhammed.

العبور إلى المنفى

أنينُ القطارِ يثيرُ شجنَ الأنفاقْ
هادراً على سكةِ الذكرياتِ الطويلة
وأنا مسمَّرٌ إلى النافذةِ
بنصف قلب
تاركاً نصفَهُ الآخرَ على الطاولة
يلعبُ البوكرَ مع فتاةٍ حسيرةِ الفخذين
تسألني بألمٍ وذهول
لماذا أصابعي متهرئة
كخشب التوابيت المستهلكة
وعجولة كأنها تخشى ألَّا تمسك شيئاً
فأحدّثها عن الوطن
واللافتات
والاستعمار
وأمجاد الأمة
والمضاجعاتِ الأولى في المراحيض
فتميلُ بشعرها النثيث على دموعي ولا تفهم
وفي الرُكنِ الآخرِ
ينثرُ موزارت توقيعاتِهِ على السهوبِ
المغطاة بالثلج...

وطني حزينٌ أكثر مما يجب
وأغنياتي جامحةٌ وشرسة وخجولة
سأمتدُّ على أولِ رصيفٍ أراه في أوربا
رافعاً ساقيَّ أمام المارة
لأريهم فلقاتِ المدارس والمعتقلات
التي أوصلتني إلى هنا
ليس ما أحمله في جيوبي جواز سفر
وإنما تأريخ قهر
حيث خمسون عاماً ونحن نجترُّ العلفَ
والخطابات....
.. وسجائر اللفِّ
حيث نقف أمام المشانق
نتطلعُ إلى جثثنا المولحة

PASSAGE TO EXILE

The train's wails awaken the tunnels' sadness
storming along rails of long-lived memories
and I am nailed to the window
with half of my heart
and the other half left behind on the table
playing poker with a young woman, her thighs half-covered
and she asks me with pain and shock
why my fingers are so lacerated
like the wood of over-used coffins and so
nervous they're afraid of holding onto anything
so I tell her about my homeland
          and the banners
                    and colonisation
and the glories of the nation
and first times of sex in latrines
then she leans her wet hair over my tears without understanding
and in the other corner
          Mozart is scattering his harmonies across moorlands
                    wrapped in snows
and my homeland is sadder than it should be
and my songs are defiant, wild and diffident
I will lay myself down on the first pavement I see in Europe
and hike my legs up to passers-by so they
will see the wheals of school beatings and detention camps
     which made me come here
What I carry in my pockets is not a passport
but a history of oppression
where for fifty years we've kept ruminating on fodder
     and speeches ...
          and hand-rolled fags
where we stand before the gallows
watching our corpses gesticulating at us

ونصفقُ للحكّام
.. خوفاً على ملفات أهلنا المحفوظةِ في أقبية الأمن
حيث الوطن
يبدأ من خطاب الرئيس
.. وينتهي بخطاب الرئيس
مروراً بشوارع الرئيس، وأغاني الرئيس، ومتاحف الرئيس، ومكارم
الرئيس ، وأشجار الرئيس ، ومعامل الرئيس، وصحف الرئيس، وإسطبل الرئيس،
وغيوم الرئيس، ومعسكرات الرئيس، وتماثيل الرئيس، وأفران الرئيس، وأنواط
الرئيس، ومحظيات الرئيس، ومدارس الرئيس، ومزارع الرئيس، وطقس الرئيس،
وتوجيهات الرئيس....
ستحدّق طويلاً
في عينيّ المبتلتين بالمطر والبصاق
وتسألني من أي بلادٍ أنا...

يوليسيس

على جسر مالمو
رأيتُ الفراتَ يمدُّ يديهِ
ويأخذني
قلتُ أينَ
ولمْ أكمل الحلمَ
حتى رأيتُ جيوشَ أمية
من كلِ صوبٍ تطوّقني

and we applaud our rulers
from fear of the dossiers on our families in the police vaults
where the homeland begins and
the homeland ends
     with the speeches of the president
And between all this the president's streets and the
     president's songs and the president's museums and
     the president's bounteousness
and the president's trees and the president's factories and
     the president's newspapers and the president's
     stables and the president's clouds and the president's
     army camps and the president's statues and the
     president's bakeries and the president's medals and
     the president's mistresses and the president's schools
     and the president's farms and the president's weather
     and the president's orders and …
She will look at me for a long time
at my eyes wet with rain and saliva
then she will ask – *What country have you come from …?*

ULYSSES

On Malmö bridge
I saw the Euphrates stretching out its hands
To carry me –
Where to? I said
And my dream couldn't end
Until I saw the Umayyad army
Besieging me from every direction.

وداعاً لنافذةٍ في بلادِ الخراب
وداعاً لسعفٍ تُجردُهُ الطائراتُ من الخضرةِ الداكنةْ
وداعاً لتنورِ أمي
وداعاً لتاريخِنا المتآكل فوق الروازين
وداعاً لما سوفَ نتركُهُ في اليدين
وداعاً
نغادرهُ الوطنَ المرَّ،
لكنْ إلى أين؟
كلُّ المنافي أمرّ ...
....

النخيلُ الذي ظلّلتني طوالعُهُ
لمْ يعدْ منه غير بقايا تصاوير شاحبةٍ
ومصاطب فارغةٍ
وجذوع مشانق ترنو لأعناقنا الحالمةْ
والفراتُ الذي عمّدتني مواجعُهُ
لمْ يزلْ سادراً بأنينِ القرى الهائمةْ
آهِ.. يوليس
ليتكَ لمْ تصل الآنَ
ليتَ الطريق إلى Malmö كانَ أبعدَ
أبعدَ
أبعدَ
أبعد
....
....

أيهذا الغريبُ الذي لمْ يجدْ لحظةً مبهجةْ
كيف تغدو المنافي سجوناً بلا أسيجةْ

مالمو 18/08/1997

84

Goodbye to a window in the land of devastation
Goodbye to the palms pared of their green by war-planes
Goodbye to my mother's clay oven
Goodbye to our history rusting on its racks
Goodbye to what may be left in our hands
Farewell
We're leaving a bitter land
But going where?
All exile is bitter …
. . . .
The palms whose helixes used to give me shade
Of them nothing's left but a pale image
Empty benches now
And their trunks, gallows for our dreaming necks
And the Euphrates whose pain baptised me
Flows on impassive past plaintive villages
O Ulysses
If you hadn't come
If only the road to Malmö were long
Long
Long
Long
. . . .
. . . .

You stranger unable to touch one instant of joy
How come all exile now is a prison without walls

Malmö 18/08/1997

العراق

العراقُ الذي يبتعدْ
كلما اتسعتْ في المنافي خطاهْ
والعراقُ الذي يتئدْ
كلما انفتحتْ نصفُ نافذةٍ..
قلتُ: آهْ
والعراقُ الذي يرتعدْ
كلما مرَّ ظلٌّ
تخيّلتُ فوّهةً تترصدني،
أو متاهْ
والعراقُ الذي نفتقدْ
نصفُ تاريخه أغانٍ وكحلٌ..
ونصفٌ طغاةْ

حزيران 1997 روتردام

أنا وهولاكو

قادني الحراسُ إلى هولاكو
كان متربعاً على عرشِهِ الفخم
وبين يديهِ حشدٌ من الوزراءِ والشعراءِ والجواري
سألني لماذا لمْ تمدحني

ارتجفتُ مرتبكاً هلعاً: يا سيدي أنا شاعرُ قصيدةِ نثر

أبتسمَ واثقاً مهيباً:
لا يهمكَ ذلك..
ثم أشارَ لسيافِهِ الأسودِ ضاحكاً:
علّمْهُ إذاً كيف يكتبُ شعراً عمودياً بشطرِ رأسِهِ
إلى شطر وعجزٍ
وإياكَ أن تخِلَّ بالوزنِ

86

IRAQ

Iraq disappears with
every step its exiles take
and contracts whenever
a window's left half-shut
and trembles wherever
shadows cross its path.
Maybe some gun-muzzle
was eyeing me up an alley.
The Iraq that's gone: half
its history was kohl and song
its other half evil, wrong.

Rotterdam 1997

ME AND HULAKU

The guards took me to Hulaku
He was sitting cross-legged on his colossal throne
A crowd of ministers, poets and slave girls before him
He asked me, 'Why haven't you sung of my glories?'

I trembled, anxious and mumbled, 'Sire, I'm but a prose poet.'

He smiled, cocksure and awesome:
'Don't let that trouble you.'
Then laughing he made a sign to the dark executioner:
'Teach him how to write columnar poetry by bisecting his head
into its first and second hemistich
and take care not to break his caesura

وإياكَ من الزحافِ والعللِ
امسكني السيافُ من ياقتي المرتجفةِ،
وهوى بسيفهِ الضخمِ
على عنقي

فتدحرجَ رأسي،
واصطدم بالنافذةِ التي انفتحتْ من هولِ الصدمة.
فاستيقظتُ هلعاً يابس الحلقِ، لأرى عنقي مبللاً بالعرق، وكتابَ الطبري ما زالَ
جاثماً على صدري، وقد اندعكت أوراقه تحت سنابكِ خيولِ هولاكو التي كانت
تنهب الممالك والقلاع، وأمامي وشيشُ التلفزيونِ الذي انتهى بثُّهُ بنهايةِ خطابِ
الرئيسِ الطويلِ
قفزتُ مرعوباً
رأيت فراشي ملطخاً بدم الكتبِ التي جرفها نهرُ دجلة، ممتزجاً بالطمي والجهشات
حاولتُ أن أجمعَ شطري رأسي اللذين التصقا بجانبي التلفزيون
وأصبحا أشبه بسماعتين يبثّانِ الوشيشَ نفسَه.

في الصباحِ........
على غيرِ العادةِ ، لم اقرأ نعيي في الجريدةِ،
ولمْ تقفْ سيارةُ الحرس أمامَ البيتِ وعليها جنازتي
ولمْ أعرفْ تفاصيلَ ما حدثَ
ذلك لأنَّ هولاكو ضجرَ من الوشيشِ
فقامَ بنفسهِ وأطفأ التلفزيونَ
وعادَ إلى كتابِ الطبريِّ ثانيةً،
مبتسماً واثقاً مهيباً،
بعد أن رفسني بخصيتي
لأنني نمتُ
قبل أن أكملَ بقيةَ سيرتِه

مالمو 01/11/1998

and beware of prosodic and metric infidelities.'
The executioner seized me by my collar
and hacked his huge sword
across my neck.

The head rolled down and struck
the window which opened at such a blow.
I woke up petrified, my throat dry, my neck wet with sweat, and
with al-Tabari's book still lying on my chest, its pages crushed
under the hooves of Hulaku's horses which were racing through
kingdoms and fortresses, and in front of me the humming of the
blank tv, the president's interminable speech gone to zero.
I jumped up petrified

Saw my bed, sullied with the blood of the books carried away
        by the Tigris, churned with mud and sobs
I tried to put my head-halves back together, but they were
        stuck like two ears on top of the TV,
As if they were the speakers broadcasting that very humming.

In the morning …
I didn't see any obituary in the papers,
the guard's car didn't stop in front of my house with my coffin on top
and I didn't get to know the details of what had happened.
That was because Hulaku got irritated with the droning
so he just upped and switched the whole racket off
and went back to al-Tabari's book,
smiling, cocksure and awesome,
having taken good care to
kick me in the balls
because I'd fallen asleep
before I'd finished
reading his histories.

Malmö 01/11/1998

89

نص

نسيتُ نفسي على طاولةِ مكتبتي
ومضيتُ
وحين فتحتُ خطوتي في الطريق
اكتشفتُ أنَّني لا شيءَ غيرُ ظلٍّ لنصٍ
أراهُ يمشي أمامي بمشقَّةٍ
ويصافحُ الناسَ كأنَّهُ أنا

مالمو 02/02/2000

كأس

في الحانة:
كانتْ بغدادُ،
خيوطَ دخان
تتصاعدُ
من أنفاسِ الجلّاسْ
وأصابع عازفةٍ، سكرى،
تتراقصُ بين الوترِ المهموسِ،
وبين الكأسْ
وإلى طاولتي، يجلسُ قلبي
ملتحفاً غصتَهُ
يرنو ولهاً للخصرِ المياسْ
ووراء زجاجِ الحانةِ أشباحٌ تترصّدني،
تحصي حولي الأنفاس
وأنا محتارٌ

TEXT

I forgot myself at my library desk
And got up to go
But as I started up the road
I realised that I was nothing but the shadow of a text
That I could see walking uneasily in front of me
And greeting people as if it were me

Malmö 02/02/2000

GLASS

It was Baghdad
    in the Bar,
        ice breaths
            rising from
                the drinkers' mouths
And the fingers of a drunk chanteuse
    dancing between the silent music
                and the glass
My heart's sat at my table
    in wrapt torment
        looking on spellbound
            at the shimmying waist
And behind the tavern windows, ghouls are watching me,
    keeping tabs on the breaths around me
        And I feel confused

‏— يا ربي —
‏أين أديرُ القلبَ؟
‏وأين أديرُ الرأسْ؟

‏مالمو 06/04/2001

مقبرة جماعية

‏منذُ عشرةِ أعوامٍ
‏تجلسُ بكاملِ فجيعتها
‏على رصيفِ أعوامها المغبرّةِ
‏في انتظارِ عودتِه
‏........
‏...
‏كلما مرَّ ظلٌّ
‏أو نعشٌ
‏تعالى شهيقُها المشروخُ
‏أعواماً تتساقطُ عن لحمِها
‏وأحلاماً مدفونةً هناك
‏........
‏الكلابُ تمرُّ أمامها، ولا تعوي
‏وكذلك رجالُ الأمنِ
‏والسياراتُ المارقة

‏أنهم يعرفونها بالتأكيد
‏لكثرةِ ما اتسعتْ عيونُهم
‏أمام سؤالها الملتاع
‏يركضُ حافياً، ويائساً

92

O Lord –
    Where to turn my heart?
            Where to turn my head?

Malmö 06/04/2001

MASS GRAVE

For ten years
She's been sitting brimful with disaster
On the roadside of her dusty seasons
Awaiting his return
. . . .
. . .
Whenever a shadow passed by
Or a coffin
Her fractured sobbing rose on high
and years fell from her skin
and her dreams, buried there
. . . .
Dogs walked in front of her without howling
Police security officers also
And their speeding cars

For sure they recognised her
Wide-eyed as they passed by
In front of her anguished questing
        that gallops, barefoot and desperate

في الطرقاتِ
والسجلاتِ
والدموع

....

لَمْ تنكثِ الترابَ...

... عن عباءتها

كأنَّ

في ذراتِه

شيئاً ئاً ئاً ئاً ئاً ئاً ئاً ئاً...

منهُ...

مالمو 20/11/2003

أوراق من سيرة تأبط منفى

1

أتسكعُ تحتَ أضواءِ المصابيحِ
وفي جيوبي عناوين مبللةٌ
حانةٌ تطردني إلى حانةٍ
وامرأةٌ تشهيني بأخرى
أعضُّ النهودَ الطازجةَ
أعضُّ الكتبَ
أعضُّ الشوارعَ
هذا الفمُ لا بدَّ أن يلتهمَ شيئاً
هذه الشفاه لا بدَّ أن تنطبقَ على كأسٍ
أو ثغرٍ
أو حجر

along roads
and archives
and tears
....
She doesn't dust down
her *abaya* ...
As if
in its specks and motes
something something something, just some little thing
might remain of him ...

Malmö 20/11/2003

PAGES FROM THE BIOGRAPHY OF AN EXILE

1

I am wandering under the street-lamps
Addresses drenched in my pocket
One tavern chases me off to another tavern
One woman's desire drives me to another woman
I bite such breasts
I bite such books
I bite such streets
This mouth must devour something
These lips must be closed over a glass
or a mouth
or a stone

لمْ يجوعني الله ولا الحقولُ
بل جوعتني الشعاراتُ
والمناجلُ التي سبقتني إلى السنابلِ

أخرجُ من ضوضائي إلى ضوضاءِ الأرصفةِ
أنا ضجرٌ بما يكفي لأن أرمي حياتي
لأيةِ عابرةِ سبيلٍ
وأمضي طليقاً
ضجراً من الذكرياتِ والأصدقاءِ والكآبةِ
ضجراً أو يائساً
كباخرةٍ مثقوبةٍ على الجرفِ
لا تستطيعُ الإقلاعَ أو الغرق

تشرين ثاني 1993 عدن

2

كتبي تحتَ رأسي
ويدي على مقبضِ الحقيبةِ
السهولُ التي حلمنا بها لمْ تمنحنا سوى الوحولِ
والكتبُ التي سطرناها لمْ تمنحنا سوى الفاقةِ والسياطِ
أقدامي احمتْ من التسكعِ على أرصفةِ الورقِ
وأغنياتي تكسّرتْ مع أقداحِ الباراتِ
ودموعي معلّقةٌ كالفوانيسِ على نوافذِ السجونِ الضيقةِ
أفردُ خيوطَ الحبرِ المتشابكةَ من كرةِ صوفِ رأسي
وأنثرها في الشوارعِ
سطراً سطراً،
حتى تنتهي أوراقي
وأنام

آذار 1996 دمشق

96

Neither God nor the fields caused me such hunger
But the slogans' propaganda did
And the sickles ahead of me taking all the spikes of wheat

I step from my own noise to the pavement's clamour
I'm bored enough to throw my life at any passing woman
And then make off unfettered
I'm bored with memories and friends and melancholy
Bored and desperate
Like a ship full of holes on the shore
Able neither to sail nor sink

Aden (Yemen) 1993

2

My books are under my head
And my hands on the handle of the suitcase
The plains we dreamt of gave us nothing but mud
And the books we wrote, poverty and lashes
My feet are eroded from hanging about on paper pavements
My songs smashed up with tavern glasses
My tears hung as lanterns from narrow prison windows
I disentangle threads of ink in my head's wool
And strew them in the streets
Line by line
Until my papers are done with
And finally I can go to sleep

Damascus 1996

3

سأحزمُ حقائبي
ودموعي
وقصائدي
وأرحلُ عن هذه البلادِ
ولو زحفتُ بأسناني
لا تطلقوا الدموعَ ورائي ولا الزغاريدَ
أريد أن أذهبَ
دون أن أرى من نوافذِ السفنِ والقطاراتِ
مناديلكم الملوحة.
أستروحُ الهواءَ في الأنفاقِ
منكسراً أمامَ مرايا المحلاتِ
كبطاقاتِ البريدِ التي لا تذهبُ لأحدٍ
لنحمل قبورنَا وأطفالَنا
لنحمل تأوهاتِنا وأحلامنَا ونمضي
قبل أن يسرقُوها
ويبيعوها لنا في الوطن: حقولاً من لافتاتٍ
وفي المنافي: وطناً بالتقسيط

هذه الأرضُ
لمْ تعدْ تصلحُ لشيءٍ
هذه الأرضُ
كلما طفحتْ فيها مجاري الدمِ والنفطِ
طفحَ الانتهازيون
أرضنا التي نتقيَّأها في الحانات
ونتركها كاللذاتِ الخاسرة
على أسِرة القحابِ
أرضنا التي ينتزعوها منا
كالجلودِ والاعترافاتِ

98

3

I will pack my suitcases
And my tears
And my poems
And leave this country for good
Even if I have to crawl using my teeth
Don't shed tears after me or ululate
I want to leave without
Looking from ship decks or train windows
At your waving handkerchiefs
I will breathe tunnel air
A broken man before shop mirrors
Send postcards that reach no-one
Let us carry our tombs and our children
Our moaning and our dreams and then leave
Before they get stolen
And resold in our homeland, as fields of billboards
Or in the places of exile, as homeland by instalment

This land
Has not been fruitful for us
Whenever torrents of blood or oil flowed over it
Opportunists also glutted the land there,
Our land, that we vomit in the taverns
And abandon as spent pleasure
                    On whores' beds,
Our land that they snatch from us
As skins and confessions

في غرفِ التحقيقِ
ويلصقونَها على اكفنا، لتصفّقَ
أمامَ نوافذِ الحكامِ

أيةُ بلادٍ هذه
ومع ذلك
ما أن نرحلَ عنها بضعَ خطواتٍ
حتى نتكسرَ من الحنين
على أولِ رصيفِ منفى يصادفنا
ونهرعُ إلى صناديقِ البريدِ
نحضنها ونبكي

كانون ثاني 1996 الخرطوم

4

حياتنا التي تشبه الضراط المتقطع في مرحاض عام
حياتنا التي لمْ يؤرخها أحد
حياتنا ناياتنا المبحوحةُ في الريح
أو نشيجنا في العلبِ
حياتنا المستهلكةُ في الأضابير
والمشرورةُ فوق حبالِ غسيلِ الحروبِ
ترى أين أوَّلي بها الآن
حين تستيقظُ فجأةً
في آخرة الليلِ
وتظلُّ تعوي في شوارعِ العالم

15/07/1999 ليلاً – قناة دوفر Dover بحر المانش

100

In interrogation chambers
And glue to our hands that we might clap
In front of our rulers' windows,
What land is this?
And in spite of this
We've only moved a few steps away
Shattered as we are with longing
On the first pavement of exile we come across
And we hurry to the post-boxes
And we hug them and we weep

Khartoum 1996

4

Our lives sputter like farts in public toilets
Our lives that no-one has chronicled
Our lives, our flutes gone hoarse in the wind
Our sobs shut up in cans
Our lives lying exhausted in dossiers
Hung out to dry on the clothes-lines of war
See, where can I go with my life now
When suddenly it wakes
At the end of night and
Keeps howling in the streets of the world?

Dover 1999

5

أضعُ يدي على خريطة العالمِ
وأحلمُ بالشوارع التي سأجوبها بقدمي الحافيتين
والخصورِ التي سأطوقها بذراعي في الحدائقِ العامةِ
والمكتباتِ التي سأستعيرُ منها الكتب ولن أعيدها
والمخبرين الذين سأراوغهم من شارعٍ إلى شارعٍ
منتشياً بالمطرِ والكركراتِ
حتى أراهم فجأةً أمامي
فأرفع إصبعي عن الخارطة خائفاً
وأنامُ ممتلئاً بالقهر

16/07/1999 حديقة الهايدبارك – لندن

6

سأقذفُ جواربي إلى السماء
تضامناً مع مَنْ لا يملكون الأحذيةَ
وأمشي حافياً
ألامسُ وحولَ الشوارع بباطنِ قدمي
محدقاً في وجوهِ المتخمَين وراءَ زجاجِ مكاتبهم
آه..
لو كانتِ الأمعاءُ البشريةُ من زجاجٍ
لرأينا كمْ سرقوا من رغيفنا
أيها الربُّ
إذا لمْ تستطعْ أن تملأَ هذه المعدةَ الجرباءَ
التي تصفرُ فيها الريحُ والديدانُ
فلماذا خلقتَ لي هذه الأضراسَ النهمة
وإذا لمْ تبرعمْ على سريري جسداً أملودا
فلماذا خلقتَ لي ذراعين من كبريت
وإذا لمْ تمنحني وطناً آمناً

102

5

I put my hand on the map of the world
And dream of the streets I will wander barefoot
Of the waists I will embrace in public gardens
Of the libraries I'll take books from and never return
Of the informers I'll evade on the streets
Elated by laughter and rains
Until suddenly I see them facing me
Then I'll lift my finger off the map, frightened
And go to sleep saturated by defeat

Hyde Park Gardens 1999

6

I'll kick my socks toward the sky
In solidarity with those who don't have shoes
And I'll walk barefoot
Feeling the mud of the streets under my feet
Staring at the faces of the glutted inside their
Glass offices,
Oh … if human intestines were glass
So we could see how much they've stolen our bread
O Lord
If You couldn't fill this starving stomach
Where worms squirm and belch
Why did you create me with these wolfing molars?
And if You didn't flesh my bed with a twig-tender body
Then why did You give me such burning arms?
And if You didn't grant me a country to be safe in

فلماذا خلقتَ لي هذه الأقدامَ الجوّابة
وإذا كنتَ ضجراً من شكواي
فلماذا خلقتَ لي هذا الفمَ المندلقَ بالصراخِ
ليلَ نهار

آب 1999 براغ

7

أين يداكَ؟
نسيتهما يلوحان للقطاراتِ الراحلةِ
أين امرأتكَ؟
اختلفنا في أوّلِ متجرٍ دخلناهُ
أين وطنُكَ؟
ابتلعتهُ المجنزرات
أين سماؤكَ؟
لا أراها لكثرةِ الدخانِ واللافتاتِ
أين حريتكَ؟
أنني لا أستطيعُ النطقَ بها من كثرةِ الارتجاف

1996 مقهى الفينيق – عمان

8

دموعي سوداء
من فرطِ ما شربتْ عيوني
من المحابرِ والزنازين
خطواتي قصيرة
من طولِ ما تعثرتْ بين السطورِ بأسلاكِ الرقيب
أمدُّ برأسي من الكتاب

104

Why did You godsend my wandering feet?
And if You grew exasperated at my complaints
Then why did You give me this mouth
Gushed with screams night and day?

Prague 1999

7

Where are your hands?
I forgot them waving to the departing trains
Where is your woman?
We argued in the first shop we stepped into
Where is your country?
Tanks have devoured it
Where is your sky?
Obscured by all the fumes and billboards
Where is your freedom?
Unspoken because I tremble so much

Amman 1996

8

My tears are black
Because my eyes have drunk
        Too much from inkwells and cells
My steps are short from such long
Stumblings through the censors' barbed wires
I crane my neck from behind my book

وأتطلعُ إلى ما خلفتُ ورائي
من شوارعَ مزدحمةٍ
وغُودٍ متأوهةٍ
ورغباتٍ مورقةٍ في الأسرّةِ
وأعجبُ كيف مرّتِ السنواتُ
وأنا مشدودٌ بخيوطِ الكلماتِ إلى ورقة

تموز 1993 مهرجان جرش- عمان

9

لا شمعة في يدي ولا حنين
فكيف أرسمُ قلبي
لا سنبلة أمامَ فمي فكيفَ أصفُ رائحةَ الشبع
لا عطور في سريري فكيف أستدلُ على جسدِ المرأة
لنستمع إلى غناءِ الملاحين
قبل أن يقلعوا بأحلامهم إلى عرضِ البحرِ وينسونا
لنستمع إلى حوارِ الأجسادِ
قبل أن ينطفئ لهاثها على الأرائك
أنا القيثارةُ مَنْ يعزفني
أنا الدموعُ مَنْ يبكيني
أنا الكلماتُ مَنْ .. يرددني
أنا الثورةُ مَنْ يشعلني

تشرين ثاني 1993 صنعاء

To see what I've left behind –
Busy streets
  Sighing breasts
    Sharp longings in the bed –
And I marvel at how the years pass by
    While I stay tied to the page with string

Amman 1993

9

No candle in my hand and no nostalgia
So how will I sketch out my heart?
No ear of wheat on my lips, so how will I depict the sweet
    smell of fullness?
No perfume in my bed, so how will I find my way to a
    woman's body?
Let's listen to the sailors' song
Before they set sail with their dreams on the high seas to forget us
Let's listen to the dialogue of bodies
Before their panting on the sofas dies down
I am the guitar, but who will play me?
I am the tears, who will mourn me?
I am the words, who will echo me?
I am the revolution, who will ignite me?

Sana'a (Yemen) 1993

10

أكتبُ ويدي على النافذة
تمسحُ الدموعَ عن وجنةِ السماء
أكتبُ وقلبي في الحقيبةِ يصغي لصفيرِ القطارات
أكتبُ وأصابعي مشتتة على مناضدِ المقاهي ورفوفِ المكتبات
أكتبُ وعنقي مشدودٌ منذ بدءِ التاريخِ
إلى حبلِ مشنقة
أكتبُ وأنا أحملُ ممحاتي دائماً
لأقلِّ طرقةِ بابٍ
وأضحكُ على نفسي بمرارةٍ
حين لا أجد أحداً
سوى الريح

1991 بغداد

11

كيف لي
أن أتخلّصَ من مخاوفي
رباه
وعيوني مسمرةٌ إلى بساطيلِ الشرطةِ
لا إلى السماءِ
وبطاقتي الشخصية معي
وأنا في سريرِ النومِ
خشيةَ أنْ يوقفني مخبرٌ في الأحلام

04/07/1999 امستردام

108

10

I write and my hand is on the window
Wiping the tears off the cheek of the sky
I write and my heart is in the suitcase listening to trains whistling
I read and my fingers skitter across café tables and library shelves
I write and my neck is tied from the outset of history
To gallows ropes
I write and my finger is always on 'delete'
For the tiniest knock at the door
And I laugh with blunt irony at myself
When I open it to nobody
But the wind

Baghdad 1991

11

How can I
Rid myself of my fears?
O God
My eyes are nailed
To police boots, not the sky and
My identity card is with me as I sleep
From fear that some informer will
Arrest me in my dreams

Amsterdam 1999

12

تحتَ سلالمِ أيامي المتآكلةِ
أجلسُ أمامَ دواتي اليابسةِ
أخططُ لمجرى قصيدتي أو حياتي
ثم أديرُ وجهي باتجاهِ الشوارعِ
ناسياً كلَّ شيءٍ
أريدُ أن أهرعَ لأولِ عمودٍ أعانقهُ وأبكي
أريدُ أن أتسكعَ تحتَ السحب العابرة
حتى تغسل آثارَ دموعي
أريد أن أغفو على أيِّ حجرٍ أو مصطبةٍ أو كتاب
دونَ أن يدقق في وجهي مخبرٌ
أو متطفلةٌ عابرةٌ
أعطوني شيئاً من الحريةِ
لأغمس أصابعي فيها
وألحسها كطفلٍ جائعٍ
أنا شاعرٌ جوّابٌ
يدي في جيوبي
ووسادتي الأرصفة
وطني القصيدة
ودموعي تفهرسُ التأريخَ
أشبحُ السنواتِ والطرقاتِ
بعجالةِ مَنْ أضاعَ نصفَ عمرِه
في خنادقِ الحروبِ الخاسرةِ والزنازين
مَنْ يغطيني من البردِ واللهاثِ ولسعاتِ العيون
وحيداً، أبتلعُ الضجرَ والوشلَ من الكؤوس المنسيّة على الطاولاتِ
وأحتكُّ بأردافِ الفتياتِ الممتلئةِ في مواقفِ الباصاتِ
لي المقاعدُ الفارغةُ
والسفرُ التي لا ينتظرها أحد
لا خبز لي ولا وطن ولا مزاج
وفي الليل
أخلعُ أصابعي

110

12

Beneath the stairs of my corroded days
I sit facing my inkwell
Planning the course of my poem or my life
Then I turn my face toward the street
And forget everything
I want to run to the nearest lamppost and hug it and weep
I want to wander under the passing clouds
Until the vestiges of my tears are washed away
I want to fall asleep on a stone or bench or book
Without any informer or passing woman
Scrutinising my face
Grant me just a morsel of freedom
To dip my fingers in, that
I might lick it like a hungry child
I am a wandering poet
My hands are in my pocket
     The pavement is my pillow
          Poems are my country
               My tears an index to history
I jump through years and pathways
In a rush, and one half of life got lost
          In the trenches of past wars, in prison cells
Who will protect me from cold and fatigue and prying eyes?
Lonely I gulp down boredom and the dregs left on bar tables
I rub myself against the buttocks of plump girls at bus stops
But the empty seats are for me
and ships that no-one wants
For me no bread, no country, no road
And at night
I pull my fingers out

وأدفنها تحتَ وسادتي
خشيةً أن أقطعها بأسناني
واحدةً بعدَ واحدة
من الجوعِ
أو الندمِ

تشرين أول 1996 بيروت

13

أيها القلبُ الضال
يا مَنْ خرجتَ حافياً ذاتَ يومٍ
مع المطرِ والسياطِ وأوراقِ الخريفِ
ولمْ تعدْ لي
سأبحثُ عنكَ
في حقائبِ الفتياتِ اللامعةِ والمواخيرِ ومحطاتِ القطاراتِ
حافياً أمرُّ في طرقاتِ طفولتي
وعلى فمي تتراكمُ دموعُ الكُتب والغبار
أجمعُ بقايا الصحفِ والغيوم الحزينة وصور الممثلات العارية
وأدلقُ وشلَ القناني الفارغةِ في جوفي
أجمعُ أعقابَ السجائر المطلية بالأحمر
وأظلُّ أحلمُ بما تركتهُ الشفاهُ الأنيقةُ من زفراتٍ
القصائدُ تتعفنُ في جيوبي
ولا أجد مَنْ ينشرها
الدموعُ تتيبسُ على شفتي
ولا أجد مَنْ يمسحها
راكلاً حياتي بقدمي من شارعٍ إلى شارع
مثلما يركلُ الطفلُ كرتَهُ الصغيرةَ ضجراً منها
وأنا...
أتأملُ وجهي في المرايا المتعاكسة

112

And hide them under my pillow
For fear I will bite them off
One by one in my sleep
Out of hunger or
From remorse

Beirut 1996

13

O you, my straying heart
You who one time went barefoot
Into the rain and lashes and autumn leaves
And still have not come back
I will look for you
In the shiny bags of young women, in the brothels and train stations
Barefoot I tramp the roads of my childhood
And accumulate in my mouth tears of books and dust
I gather the remnant of newspapers, sad clouds and
          pictures of naked actresses
And pour the left-over dregs into my empty belly
I collect red-stained cigarette butts
And dream of the sighs left behind by elegant lips
Poems become mouldy in my pockets
No-one will publish them
Tears go dry on my lips and
No-one wipes them away
I'm kicking my life from street to street
As a small child kicks his ball out of boredom
And I ...
I contemplate my face in the mirror's reflection

وأعجبُ
كيف هرمتُ
بهذه العجالة

07/01/2000 أوسلو

14

سأجلسُ على بابِ الوطنِ محدودبَ الظهرِ
كأغنيةٍ حزينةٍ تنبعثُ من حقلٍ فارغٍ
يغطيني الثلجُ وأوراقُ الشجرِ اليابسةُ
أنظرُ إلى أسرابِ العائدين من منافيهم كالطيورِ المتعبةِ
أمسحُ عن أجفانهم الثلوجَ والغربةَ
إنهم يعودون...
لكن مَنْ يعيد لهم ما ضيعوهُ
من رملٍ وأحلامٍ وسنوات

أقلعتُ في أولِ قطارٍ إلى المنفى
وأنا أفكرُ بالعودة
شاختْ سكةُ الحديدِ
وتهرأتِ العجلاتُ
وامحّتْ ثيابي من الغسيلِ
وأنا ما زلتُ مسافراً في الريحِ
أتطايرُ بحنيني في قاراتِ العالَم
مثل أوراقِ الرسائلِ الممزقةِ
دموعي مكسّرةٌ فَي الباراتِ
وأصابعي ضائعةٌ على مناضدِ المقاهي
تكتبُ رسائلَ الحنينِ
لأصدقائي الذين لا أملكُ عناوينهم
أنامُ على سطوحِ الشاحناتِ
وعيوني المغرورقةٌ باتجاهِ الوطنِ البعيد

114

And I am astonished
At how I have grown old
In so short a time

Oslo 2000

14

I'll sit hunchbacked by the gates of my motherland
Like a sad song rising from an empty field
Snow and dry leaves will sheath me
As I look at the emigrants flocking back from exile like
       exhausted birds
And I'll wipe from their eyelids the snows of estrangement
It is true, they are returning ...
But who will give them back what they've lost
       Of sand and dreams and years

I set sail in the first train for exile
Already thinking of my return
The rail tracks have aged
And the wheels are worn down
And my clothes are discoloured from washing
And still I'm travelling with the wind
Flying with my longing across the continents
Like pieces of shredded letters
My tears scattered in bars
My fingers disappearing on café tables
Writing letters of longing to friends whose addresses I'd lost
I sleep on truck roofs

كطائرٍ لا يدري على أيِّ غصنٍ يحطُّ
لكنني دون أن أتطلعَ من نافذةٍ القطارِ العابرِ سهوب وطني
أعرفُ ما يمرُّ بي
من أنهارٍ
وزنازين
ونخيلٍ
وقرىً. أحفظها عن ظهرِ قلبٍ
سأرتمي، في أحضانِ أولِ كومةِ عشبٍ تلوحُ لي من حقولِ بلادي
وأمرِّغُ فمي بأوحالها وتوتها وشعاراتها الكاذبةِ
لكنني
لن أطرقَ البابَ يا أمي
إنهم وراء الجدران ينتظرونني بنصالهم اللامعة
لا تنتظري رسائلي
إنهم يفتشون بين الفوارز والنقاطِ عن كلِّ كلمةٍ أو نأمةٍ
فاجلسي أمامَ النافذة
واصغي في الليلِ إلى الريح
ستسمعين نجوى روحي

1998 مالمو

15

خطوطُ يدي امحت من التشبّثِ بالريحِ والأسلاك
ومن العاداتِ السرّيةِ
مع نساء لا أعرفهن
التقطتهنَّ بسنّارة أحلامي من الشارع
وهذه الشروخ، التي ترينها ليستْ سطوراً
بل آثار المساطر التي انهالتْ على كفي
وهذه الندوب، عضّات أصابعي

116

My eyes are bathed in tears for my far-off land
Like a bird not knowing on which branch to alight
But I know what is there without looking from the train
Over the steppes to my motherland
What passes by of rivers,
Of dungeons, date palms and villages
I know them all by heart
And I'll fall into the arms of the first heap of grass
Waving to me from the fields of my country
And rub my face in its muds and mulberries and false slogans
But I won't
Knock at the door, my mother
They'll be waiting behind the walls with shining blades
So don't wait for my letters
They'll search through every word and whisper, all the
            commas and full-stops,
So sit in front of the window
And listen to the winds at night:
You'll hear my soul's soliloquy

Malmö 1998

15

The lines on my palms have been erased from clinging fast
To the wind and barbed wire
And from masturbating with unknown women
I picked up from the streets with the fish-hook of dreams
And these cracks that you see are not lines
But traces of the rulers that rained blows on my palms
And these scars, from biting my own fingers

من الندم والغضب والارتجاف
فلا تبحثي عن طالعي في راحتي
– ياسيدتي العرافة –
ما دمتُ مرهوناً بهذا الشرقِ
فمستقبلي في راحات الحكام

20/03/1990 كورنيش النيل– القاهرة

16

لا أعرفُ متى سأسقطُ على رصيفِ قصائدي
مكوّماً بطلقة
أو مثقوباً من الجوع
أو بطعنةَ صديق
يمرُّ الحكامُ والأحزابُ والعاهراتُ
ولا يد تعتُّ بياقتي وتنهضني من الركامِ
لا عنق يستديرُ نحوي
ليرى كيفَ يشخبُ دمي كساقيةٍ على الرصيفِ
لا مشيعين يحملونني متأففين إلى المقبرة
الأقدامُ تدوسني أو تعبرني
وتمضي
الفتياتُ يشحنَ بأنظارهن
وهن يمضغن سندويشاتهن ونكاتهن المدرسية البذيئة
ومئذنةُ الجامع الكبير
تصاعدُ تسابيحها – ليلَ نهار –
دون أن تلتفت لجعيري
....
لا أعرفُ على أيِّ رصيفِ منفى
ستسّاقطُ أقدامي ورموشي من الانتظار
لا أعرفُ أيَّ أظافرٍ نتنةٍ ستمتدُ إلى جيوبي
وتسلبني قصائدي

118

From remorse and anger and trembling
So don't seek my future from the palm of my hand
Good lady, good fortune-teller
Because it's pawned in these eastern lands
My future is in the hands of the rulers

Cairo 1990

16

I don't know when I'll collapse, gunned down
In a heap on the pavement of my poems,
Or punctured by hunger
          Or stabbed by a friend
They pass by, rulers, party members, prostitutes
But no hand yanks me by the collar and pulls me from the heap
No head turns towards me to see
How my blood flows like a little stream on the pavement
No hired mourners carry me, grumbling, to the cemetery
Feet step on me or wade through me
Then pass by
Girls avert their glances
As they bite on their sandwiches and dirty school jokes
And the minaret of the big mosque
Sends its prayers up, night and day,
Without paying any attention to my braying
. . . .
I don't know on which pavement of exile
My feet will collapse, my eyelashes droop from waiting
I don't know whose rotting nails will slip into my pockets
To steal my poems

ومحبرتي وأحلامي
في وضح النهار
لا أعرفُ على أيِّ سريرِ فندقٍ أو مستشفى
سأستيقظ
لأجد وسادتي خاليةً...
ودموعي باردةً
ووطني بعيد
لا أعرفُ في أيِّ منعطفِ جملةٍ أو وردةٍ
سيسدد أحدهم طعنتَهُ المرتبكةَ العميقةَ
إلى ظهري
من أجلِ قصيدةٍ كتبتها ذاتَ يومٍ
أشتمُ فيها الطغاة والطراطير
ومع ذلك سأواصلُ طوافي وقهقهاتي وشتائمي
عابراً وليس لي غير الأرصفةِ والسعالِ الطويلِ
ليس لي غير الحبرِ والسلامِ والأمطارِ
سائراً مثلَ جنديٍ وحيدٍ
يجُرُّ بين الأنقاضِ حياتَهُ الجريحةَ
لا أريدُ أوسمةً ولاَ طبولاً ولا جرائدَ
أريدُ أن أضعَ جبيني الساخنَ
على طينِ أنهارِ بلادي
وأموت حالماً كالأشجار

برلين 11/11/2000

120

And my inkpot and my dreams
In the full light of day
I don't know in which hotel or hospital bed
I'll wake up
To find an empty pillow ...
And my tears cold
And my motherland far away
I don't know into which whorl of words or rose
Someone will aim a deep, bewildered stab
Into my back
Because of some poem I wrote
Cursing tyrants and buffoons
And in spite of this I will go on wandering and guffawing and
        cursing
And wading through nothing but pavements and hacking
        coughs
There is nothing for me but ink and stairs and rain
Walking like a lone soldier
Who drags his wounded life through the rubble
I don't want medals or drum-calls or public praise
I just want to lay my fevered forehead
On the silt of my country's rivers
And to die there as trees do.

Berlin 2000

سأعبرُ؛ شوارعَ القصيدةِ، حافياً
وحيداً
أتسوّلُ الأحلامَ من الكتبِ والارصفة
وأتلمّظُ القبلاتِ من شفاهِ العابراتِ
ملوّحاً بذراعيَّ الذابلتين
لسنواتي التي تُجهشُ بمقاعدها الفارغة
للرفوفِ التي تتجحشّأُ أمامي التعاليمَ والتبنَ والذكرياتِ
لصهيلِ الصدورِ النافرةِ، خلف النوافذِ الموصدةِ
أيامي تتخاصم مع بعضها
وأصابعي تضجر من يدي
أرنو إلى الطيورِ
وهي تنكشُ شَعَرَ الغيومِ بمناقيرها
أرنو إلى القُبلِ التي انفرطت، على عشب الحدائق
دونَ أنْ تصلَ....
أرنو إلى المقاهي
حيثُ تتلامسُ تحت طاولاتها أفخاذُ العشاقِ الملتاعةُ
ولا أجدُ من تلامسني
فأفتحُ صرتي، في الليلِ،
لأمضغَ أحلامي علىَ السريرِ
وأصابعي
تحتضنُ
ي ر ا عـ...
....   ي

أين أجدكَ أيها القلبُ الضال
في هذا الخريفِ الموحشِ
لأعضَّكَ وأبكي

هذه الليلةَ لنْ أنام
وذراعاي وحيدتان

17

I will walk the streets of the poem,
Barefoot and alone
Begging dreams from books and pavements
Licking kisses from the lips of passing women
Waving my arms exhausted
From years of sobbing on empty sofas
From shelves belching doctrines, chaff, memories at me,
From the whinnying of young bodies behind shut windows.
My days quarrel with each other
And my fingers are angry with my hands.
I consider the birds
They are ruffling the clouds' hair with their beaks
I consider the kisses dissolved on the lawns of the gardens,
Before they've begun ...
I consider the cafes
Where lovers' burning legs touch beneath tables
But no-one is touching me
I open my bag in the night
So I can savour my dreams on the bed
And my fingers
Close round
M-y-y-y b-i-i-i- ...
                ... r-r-r-r-d-d-d-d

Where will I find you, O straying heart
In this desolate autumn
To take you in my teeth and lament

Tonight I will not sleep
And my arms are lonely

سأحتسي أيَّ سحابةٍ أو دمعةٍ
إنْ لمْ أجدْ كأساً
سأضمُّ أيَّ عمودٍ إلى صدري
إنْ لمْ أجدْ خصراً

11/10/2008 كاليكري – كندا

الحلاج، ثانيةً

مَنْ ينقذني من بلواي
ما في الجبةِ إلاّهُ
وما في الجبةِ إلاّيْ
وأنا الواحدُ
وهو الواحدُ
كيفَ اتحدا
كيف انفصلا
في لحظةِ سكرٍ
بين شكوكي فيهِ
وتقواي

2004 لندن

I'll slurp up every last cloud, and every tear
        If I don't find a glass
I'll hug every lamppost
        If I can't find a waist

Calgary (Canada) 2008/10/11

AL-HALLAJ AGAIN

Who will deliver me?
No-one in a Jubbah but He,
No-one in a Jubbah but Me,
I am the One
He is the One and Only
How were we spasmed together,
How were we rent apart?
In a moment of drink
Between my doubting Him
And my piety?
How would I know?

London 2004

تهجدات

....

لم تَرَ رَبَّكَ
إلاَّ بالنصلِ
وبالدمِّ
وأنا أبصرهُ...
في الكَلِمةِ
في النغمةِ
في زرقةِ عينيها،
... واليَمْ

....

*

آياتٌ
نسختْ
آياتْ
وتريدُ لرأسِكَ أنْ يبقى
جلموداً
لا يتغيرُ والسنواتْ

....

*

يا هذا الفانْ
ولتنظرْ
كيف تحاورَ ربُّكَ والشيطانْ
أكثيرٌ أنْ تتعلمَ
كيف تحاورُ انسانْ

....

*

126

NIGHT PRAYERS

....

You see
    your God only
            in blades and blood
I perceive Him ...
            in a word
            and a song
and in the blue of her eyes
            and the sea ...

....

        *

verses
have annulled
verses
and you want your head
rock-hard and
unchanged through the years

....

        *

you who are a man
consider
how you talk with your Lord and the devil
Is it then too much to hope you'd learn
how to talk with your fellow men?

        *

لا ناقوسَ
ولا مئذنةٌ
يا عبدُ –
لماذا
لا تسمعُ
ربَّكَ
في
الناي

2004 لندن

ربي واحدْ

لا كاثوليكيٌّ   لا بروستانتيٌّ
لا سنيٌّ   لا شيعيٌّ
مَنْ جزّأهُ
مَنْ أوَّلهُ
مَنْ قوَّلهُ
من صنَّفهُ
وفقَ مذاهبهِ،
ومطالبهِ،
ومصالحهِ،
ودساترهِ،
وعساكرهِ،
فهو الجاحدْ

2004 لندن

no bell or
minaret
– O Servant of God
why
won't you
hear your
Lord
in a
flute ?

London 2004

MY GOD IS ONE

Neither Catholic   nor Protestant
        neither Shi'a   nor Sunni
whoever bisected
                whoever dissected
                        whoever deliberated
                                whoever segregated
                                        and so disintegrated
                                it's their aims
                        their interests
                their laws and
        their armies
they're the ones who lack all faith!

London 2004

ADNAN AL-SAYEGH was born in al-Kufa, Iraq in 1955. One of the most original voices of the generation of Iraqi poets that came to maturity in the 1980s, his poetry, sharp and crafted with elegance, carries an intense passion for freedom, love and beauty. His words denounce the devastation of wars and the horrors of dictatorship, but also act on quieter and more personal levels. In the 1980s he was conscripted in the Iran-Iraq War and in 1993 his uncompromising criticism of oppression and injustice led to exile in Jordan and the Lebanon. In 1996 he published *Uruk's Anthem*, a book-length poem – one of the longest in Arabic literature – in which he richly articulates deep despair at the Iraqi experience. On its publication he was sentenced to death in Iraq and took refuge in Sweden. Since 2004 has been living in exile in London.

Eleven collections of his poetry in Arabic, among them *Formations, Uruk's Anthem* and *Carrying his Exile Under his Arm*, have been published and a further one is in production. The poems translated in the present volume recognise the trajectory of his exile and the concerns of his life.

Adnan al-Sayegh has received several international awards, including the Hellman-Hammet International Poetry Award (New York, 1996), the Rotterdam International Poetry Award (1997) and the Swedish Writers Association Award (2005). His poetry has been translated into many languages and he is frequently invited to take part in poetry festivals around the world.

STEPHEN WATTS is a poet, editor & translator. Among his own most recent books are *Mountain Language / Lingua di montagna* (2008) & *Journey Across Breath / Tragitto nel respire* (2011) (both published by Hearing Eye and with Italian translation by Cristina Viti), *Ancient Sunlight* (Enitharmon,

2014) and *Republic Of Dogs / Republic Of Birds* (Test Centre, 2016). Among his co-translations are chapbooks by Ziba Karbassi and Adnan al-Sayegh, *All My Young Years* by A. N. Stencl, *Ljubljana* by Meta Kušar and anthologies of Slovenian & Kurdish poetry. He edited Amarjit Chandan's *Sonata For Four Hands* for Arc Publications in 2010 and is currently is working on translations of Tonino Guerra, Victor Sunyol, a full length collection of Ziba Karbassi's poetry and the anthology *Six Georgian Poets* (forthcoming from Arc). He has been poet in residence in schools and hospitals, runs a poetry workshop at a drop-in centre in Islington and researches issues of language, creativity, well-being and migration. He has lived since 1977 in Whitechapel and has been strongly involved with Bangladeshi culture in East London. He has read his own work internationally, most recently in Sibiu, Bucharest, Milan and Ravenna. In 2010 he read at festivals in Syria & works closely with the Syrian poet Golan Haji who lives now in Paris.

MARGA BURGUI-ARTAJO was born in Navarra in the north of Spain and initially studied chemistry. Always an avid reader and in conscious reaction against an education experienced under Franco, she began to study Arabic in 1981, partly to recover for herself some of the roots of her own Hispanic culture, and partly after reading Juan Goytisolo. Since 1994 she has lived permanently in London and has worked at Paddington Library where she established a substantial holding of both classical and contemporary Arabic literature, and where she also came into closer contact with London-based Arabic writers and bookshops. At present she works with a diverse range of cultural groups across and beyond London.